Praise for *The EduProtocol Field Guide*

The EduProtocol Field Guide: Primary Edition expertly bridges the traditional and digital worlds by pairing time-tested educational strategies with platforms and apps tailored for primary learners. The authors are wonderful teachers who skillfully model how to thoughtfully establish classroom culture and meaningfully engage young pupils through innovative structures that mirror real-world communication and collaboration.

—**Sean M. Arnold,** director of School Pathways, NYC Public Schools

Simply put, this book is AWESOME. It's going to make a huge impact in classrooms with kids and teachers!

—**Adam Welcome,** author, keynote speaker, and podcaster

This book provides educators with replicable, low-prep protocols that make academic content accessible to young learners while ensuring the opportunity for students to create, communicate, collaborate, and think critically. The result is decreased busywork for teachers and increased engagement from students.

—**Adam Juárez and Katherine Goyette,** educators, leaders, and authors

The authors demonstrate a profound understanding of the importance of classroom culture, exploration, joy, and celebration in creating a dynamic learning environment adaptable to any instructional strategy.

—**Cate Tolnai,** director of digital learning, SBCEO

Imagine classrooms where each lesson is a magical brushstroke on the canvas of a student's intellectual and creative growth. Jenn and Ben have created a masterpiece for primary teachers!

—**Dr. Natasha Rachell,** director of instructional technology, Atlanta Public Schools

In this day and age where teachers are finding it more complicated than ever before to differentiate for the wide variety of needs of their students, Ben and Jenn have done a fantastic job of providing examples and information that will make differentiation as well as scaffolding and engagement easier than ever. Their examples are clear, simple to follow, and will help any teacher to build a strong culture.

—**Kelly May-Vollmar, EdD,** superintendent

This is a resource full of strategies and ideas that you will keep within easy reach and refer to often when designing magical learning experiences in your classroom. Highly recommend!

—**Tisha Richmond,** educational consultant, international speaker, author

Benjamin Cogswell and Jennifer Dean seamlessly blend innovation and practicality to build culture and community, and inspire a dynamic shift in students' learning experiences. Teachers will appreciate the detailed guides on how to use EduProtocols in addition to the treasure trove of supplementary resources and student samples in the Extended Content links.

—**Stacey L. Joy, NBCT,** fifth-grade teacher

This book is a must-have for any primary educator looking to instill ownership of learning within their classrooms through dynamic and meaningful learning experiences.

—**Lisa Moe,** teacher

This book allows for our K-2 students to build cognitive routines that make learning "sticky" and accessible. These lesson frames provide students the support to be independent learners that in turn rewards the teacher with more time to cultivate learning partnerships with students.

—**Dr. Nyree Clark,** coordinator of equity and access

Wow! I am so excited for primary teachers to discover they can "teach better, work less, and achieve more"!

—**Kimberly DeMille,** intervention specialist

This book is a must-read for every primary educator seeking to improve and enhance student engagement and who believes in what our littlest learners *can* do!

—**Susan Stewart,** teacher and technology integration specialist

What truly sets this book apart is its seamless integration into the classroom for primary learners, adaptable across tech spectrums—be it no-tech, low-tech, or high-tech platforms like Seesaw.

—**Lisa Nowakowski,** author and technology teacher on special assignment

Having Ben and Jenn's resources at my fingertips will certainly help me make learning better for my students. Their book is like a direct line for support while planning a solid literacy and numeracy base for our students.

—**Kimberly Voge,** author and computer literacy TOSA

This guide offers a wealth of practical strategies, classroom-tested frameworks, and innovative approaches to engage students of all learning styles.

—**Chrystal Hoe,** teacher

As a longtime teacher of "littles" and champion of EduProtocols, I have dreamed of a primary edition developed for our youngest learners. My students love using MathReps to practice math facts and Random Emoji to generate fun and creative sentences. The lesson frames from this book help boost my student engagement and academic performance while improving my teaching experience. I encourage all primary teachers to use EduProtocols to teach better, work less, and achieve more.

—**Garrick MacDonald,** first-grade teacher, Oakhurst Elementary, Oakhurst, CA

The EduProtocol Field Guide: Primary Edition

Bring Your Teaching into Focus

THE EduProtocol
FIELD GUIDE
Primary Edition

— 5 —
Lesson Frames for TK-2
Plus Start-up Guidance

Benjamin Cogswell & Jennifer Dean
with Marlena Hebern & Jon Corippo
Foreword by Catlin R. Tucker

The EduProtocol Field Guide Primary Edition: 5 Lesson Frames for TK–2 Plus Start-up Guidance
© 2024 Benjamin Cogswell, Jennifer Dean, Marlena Hebern, and Jon Corippo

All rights reserved. No part of this publication may be reproduced in any form or by any electronic or mechanical means, including information storage and retrieval systems, without permission in writing by the publisher, except by a reviewer who may quote brief passages in a review. For information regarding permission, contact the publisher at books@daveburgess-consulting.com.

> This book is available at special discounts when purchased in quantity for educational purposes or for use as premiums, promotions, or fundraisers. For inquiries and details, contact the publisher at books@daveburgessconsulting.com.

Published by Dave Burgess Consulting, Inc.
San Diego, CA
DaveBurgessConsulting.com

Library of Congress Control Number: 2023951247
Paperback ISBN: 978-1-956306-69-9
Ebook ISBN: 978-1-956306-70-5

Cover and interior design by Liz Schreiter
Edited and produced by Reading List Editorial
ReadingListEditorial.com

Ben's Dedication

I'd like to dedicate this book to my family: Jenny, Sunny, Russell, Tucker, Jamison, Grandpa Ben, Grandma Dolly, Nana, G.G., Meghan, John, and my loyal adventure companion, Koko. You have always believed in me! Thanks for the support along the way.

Jenn's Dedication

This book is dedicated to my family, who has helped make this dream come true! And to my son, Jack: I hope this accomplishment encourages you to follow your dreams as well!

Contents

1	Foreword
5	**Section 1: Introduction**
6	Chapter 1: Let's Get It Started!
12	Chapter 2: Why EduProtocols?
18	Chapter 3: Why Seesaw?
22	**Section 2: Smart Start**
23	Chapter 4: Building Culture
41	Chapter 5: Technology
49	Chapter 6: Starting with Seesaw
53	Chapter 7: Classroom Introduction to Smart Start
59	**Section 3: EduProtocols**
60	Chapter 8: Little p*ARTS EduProtocol
73	Chapter 9: Little Random Emoji Writing EduProtocol
88	Chapter 10: Fast and Curious EduProtocol
102	Chapter 11: MathReps EduProtocol
113	Chapter 12: Sketch and Tell EduProtocol
129	Chapter 13: Racking and Stacking EduProtocols
140	**Section 4: Smart Start EduProtocols**
141	Chapter 14: Smart Start: Fast and Curious EduProtocol
149	Chapter 15: Smart Start: Sketch and Tell EduProtocol
158	Chapter 16: Smart Start: MathReps EduProtocol
167	Chapter 17: Final Thoughts and Call to Action
169	Want to Learn More about Using EduProtocols in Your Classroom?
170	Citations
171	Acknowledgments
173	About the Authors
175	More from Dave Burgess Consulting, Inc.

Foreword

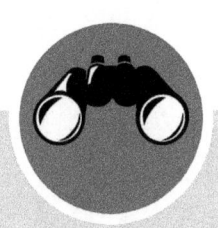

Coaching elementary teachers in K–5 classrooms introduced me to a new world of working closely with incredible little minds. Stepping into those classrooms, filled with energetic, affectionate, and endlessly curious students, starkly contrasted my previous experience teaching high school English. But within the vibrant and colorful walls of elementary classrooms, I discovered a profound joy in working with these young learners. The greatest challenge of designing and facilitating new learning experiences for elementary students is the onboarding process—introducing these tiny humans to new routines, procedures, activities, and instructional models. It required meticulous planning and relentless practice, yet witnessing the astounding capabilities of even the youngest students, guided by their dedicated and patient teachers, was nothing short of awe-inspiring.

Throughout my twenty-two-year career in education, I have worn numerous hats, including those of a teacher, coach, author, and speaker. I am deeply committed to the transformative power of shifting from traditional teacher-led instruction to student-centered instructional models. However, I have encountered skepticism about students' ability to thrive in such environments, particularly among educators working with younger students.

The fear of relinquishing control and granting students more autonomy and agency in the classroom can be daunting. There are genuine concerns about the students' ability to manage their behavior effectively and make responsible decisions. However, teachers must take a proactive approach to developing self-directed learners instead of allowing these fears to hinder progress and stifle innovation. It is our responsibility to guide and support students as they develop the necessary skills and confidence to become active agents in their learning journeys.

Jenn Dean and Ben Cogswell's early elementary version of EduProtocols presents a unique and invaluable resource for educators seeking to unlock the full potential of their primary-grade classrooms. EduProtocols are versatile and flexible lesson frames that enable educators to seamlessly integrate curriculum content, effectively deliver instruction, and maintain a low cognitive load for students. The book highlights the importance of building a positive classroom culture, establishing clear procedures, and implementing a Smart Start approach to ensure a smooth and successful implementation of EduProtocols.

What sets this book apart is its progressive, practical, and edtech-friendly approach tailored to young learners. By adapting these established EduProtocols to the primary grades, the authors have created a systematic and accessible framework that dramatically increases student engagement and promotes the development of twenty-first-century skills.

Within these pages, teachers will discover a comprehensive guide to implementing EduProtocols effectively in TK–2 classrooms. The book provides step-by-step instructions, practical tips, and real-life examples to help educators integrate EduProtocols into their curriculum, cultivating a dynamic and interactive learning environment. With the inclusion of brand-new EduProtocols designed specifically for primary grades, teachers will have a rich toolkit of strategies.

By embracing EduProtocols in early classrooms, teachers can create a student-centered classroom where young learners become active agents driving learning in classrooms. The book empowers teachers to harness the power of the Four Cs of twenty-first-century learning and effectively incorporate them into daily instruction. Using EduProtocols will help students develop confidence in their ability to solve problems, work with diverse groups of peers, and think creatively.

This book also addresses the challenges of utilizing technology in primary classrooms by showcasing how Seesaw, a digital student engagement platform, can help teachers seamlessly integrate EduProtocols into the classroom. However, it's important to note that the principles and strategies discussed can be applied to other online learning platforms or traditional paper-based approaches, ensuring accessibility and flexibility for educators.

The goal of technology should be to minimize complexity, maximize individual potential, and enhance relationships within the learning community, which EduProtocols strive to do! This technology-friendly approach ensures that teachers can confidently incorporate digital tools into their lessons, fostering digital literacy and strategically using technology to enhance students' ability to think critically, communicate, collaborate, and create.

The elementary version of EduProtocols is an indispensable resource for primary-grade educators who strive to create a dynamic, inclusive learning environment that sets the stage for academic success and lifelong learning. By following the guidance provided in this book, teachers can add a robust collection of practical strategies and innovative ideas to their teaching toolboxes to transform their classrooms into dynamic, student-centered learning communities.

Catlin R. Tucker

Dr. Catlin R. Tucker is a best-selling author, keynote speaker, international trainer, and professor in the Master of Arts in Teaching program at Pepperdine University. She taught for sixteen years in Sonoma County, where she was named Teacher of the Year in 2010.

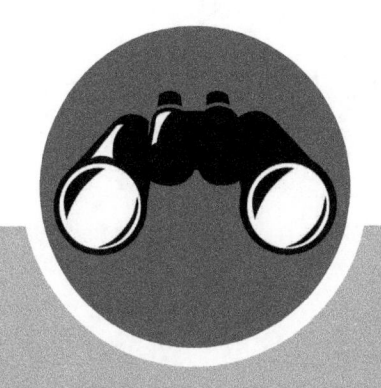

SECTION 1
Introduction

Chapter 1
Let's Get It Started!

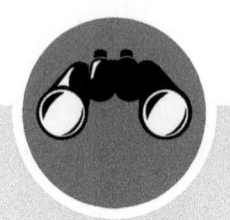

Welcome to the EduProtocol Field Guide for our youngest learners. This book has been in the making for a few years, and we are happy that you finally have it in your hands.

As a primary teacher, you have no doubt been to a training and thought, "That strategy is great, but how can I make it work for primary grades?" Well, this book is for you! In *The EduProtocol Field Guide Primary Edition*, we take the EduProtocols and explain how we apply them successfully to primary grades. Of course, just for fun, we've added a few new variations to some familiar EduProtocols just for the primary grades.

Let us introduce ourselves: we are Jennifer Dean and Ben Cogswell.

Jenn is currently a first-grade teacher in Southern California. Jenn has masters degrees in early childhood education and instructional technology, has experience from preschool to second grade, and has been teaching nine years. Jenn started her educational career as a paraprofessional and became a teacher. She started teaching in Illinois, then moved to California and started teaching there in the 2016–2017 school year.

Ben has been teaching kindergarten for the last several years in central California. Ben started teaching in 2007 and is currently in his seventeenth year of teaching. His journey has taken him from being a sixth-grade teacher to an educational technology coach to teaching in the kinder classroom. Over the years, Ben has developed

> **Marlena & Jon**
>
> You don't have to read this book cover to cover. Feel free to jump around, skip sections, and come back to the EduProtocols that you need.

a passion for using technology with a hands-on learning approach to promote language and literacy skills in students.

Both of us have been implementing EduProtocols in our primary classrooms for several years. We were drawn to them pretty quickly because as primary teachers we understand the importance of repetition to help students be successful, and EduProtocols are all about the reps. Additionally, if you have ever heard us speak, we are always emphasizing the importance of building language with our students. EduProtocols implement the Four Cs (critical thinking, communication, collaboration, and creativity), which helps students build so much language and creates an amazing classroom culture. As we have grown as educators implementing EduProtocols in our classrooms, we have seen our students grow and accomplish more than we could imagine. Each year it gets better, and we can really dive deeper into more protocols. That is why we are so excited that, with the help of Marlena Hebern and Jon Corippo, we are bringing you this book.

What Are EduProtocols?

EduProtocols are lesson frames into which you will insert your curriculum to teach more effectively and deliver more engaging content. By using the same lesson frames while moving through content, we keep the cognitive load low on students. In the primary grades, it is important to provide students with a familiar structure so they can focus on learning the content rather than how to complete different templates.

As frames, EduProtocols are adaptable as the curriculum changes and students move from one topic to another. Once students have learned a particular lesson frame, the teacher is able to repeat that lesson frame again and again with a variety of content throughout the year. This allows for students to gain familiarity with a process that can be used repeatedly for different learning goals.

EduProtocols also lean on several best practices, including the Four Cs (collaboration, critical thinking, communication, and creativity) in a format that incorporates Universal Design for Learning

Jenn

Using EduProtocols made me a better teacher. I was able to differentiate instruction more effectively, meet the needs of my diverse learners, and see huge growth even on my i-Ready scores.

Ben

I love blended learning, using both manipulatives and technology. EduProtocols allow me to do just this. My students get to experience the best of both worlds and have more voice and choice in their learning.

If you want to learn more about our journeys, you can visit this webpage.

primaryeduprotocols.us/authors

(UDL). Not all of the EduProtocols tap into all of the Four C skills, but most do at varying levels. You can find detailed information about the Four Cs in chapter 14, "The Four Cs Throwdown," in *The EduProtocol Field Guide, Book 1*.

EduProtocols allow for teachers to differentiate their instruction to meet the needs of their diverse students almost seamlessly. Since they offer so much repetition, the students who learn them quickly can start to use them independently while the teacher works in a small group with other students who need a little more assistance. Additionally, they allow students to work at their own level while getting immediate feedback. For example, you may be running the EduProtocol Little p*ARTS in your classroom. Some students will start naming more advanced nouns like *reptile*, whereas other students may just name the noun *snake*. Both are correct, but students are not limited by their language knowledge. Instead, all students are able to be successful.

EduProtocols are suitable for students across all grades. In this book, though, Ben, Jenn, Marlena, and Jon have taken the traditional format of the EduProtocols and adapted them to make them more effective at the TK–2 level. We have also included many tips to make deploying EduProtocols with young students seamless for the teacher, because in the end, we want you to enjoy teaching, and we want students to crave learning!

As we resituate EduProtocols for TK–2 learners, we will challenge students to dig deeper while keeping the technology skill level for teachers streamlined. Most EduProtocols use Google Slides or PowerPoint as the foundation, and in this book, we will show you how to use paper and Seesaw to leverage the Four Cs in your young students.

Connections to Standards

Each EduProtocol is designed to support more than one standard. For example, in a Sketch and Tell, students may read a paragraph about elephants (RI 1.10) and be asked a specific question such as "What do elephants eat?" and sketch their answer (RI 1.1 and SL

1.5). Then they take turns speaking and listening and using complete sentences when telling their partner about their sketch (SL 1.6). After taking turns with their partner(s), students answer the specific question (RI 1.1) by writing a complete sentence (L 1.1).

The standards contained in a particular EduProtocol can be shaped by the teacher, depending on the directions and focus of the instruction. Use the chart on page 10 to guide you, but as you learn each EduProtocol, be open to its possibilities!

How to Use This Book

We've worked hard to get you started with EduProtocols, but this book also offers much more. In fact, as we wrote this book, we packed in *so* much more that we decided we couldn't contain it all in a single book. Therefore, we have created a whole resource that lives outside this book, which we will refer to as our "Extended Content."

The Extended Content section is extra awesome because it can grow and change as the technology we use changes. Make sure you bookmark the page for the Extended Content section and note the password: **73468**.

Extended Content:
Table of Contents

Our digital **Table of Contents** is your one stop shop for all the extended content in this book. It is password protected because we value you. The password is **73468**.

In the extended content, you'll get:
- ★ Smart Start section including Why We Love Seesaw, Building Culture, Logging in & Device Care, and Starting with Seesaw
- ★ EduProtocols Little p*PARTS, Emoji Writing, Fast & Curious, MathReps, and Sketch and Tell
- ★ Other awesome templates and resources

tinyurl.com/eppewebsite
Password: 73468

Kindergarten Common Core Standards

Standard	Description	Little Parts	Random Emoji	FAC	Math Reps	SKAT
ELA-LITERACY.L.K.1.B	Use frequently occurring nouns and verbs.	✓				✓
ELA-LITERACY.L.K.1.F	Produce and expand complete sentences in shared language activities.	✓				✓
ELA-LITERACY.RF.K.3.A	Demonstrate basic knowledge of one-to-one letter-sound correspondences by producing the primary sound or many of the most frequent sounds for each consonant.		✓			✓
ELA-LITERACY.L.K.2.D	Spell simple words phonetically, drawing on knowledge of sound-letter relationships.		✓			✓
ELA-LITERACY.L.K.1.F	Produce and expand complete sentences in shared language activities.		✓			✓
ELA-LITERACY.RF.K.3.A	Basic knowledge of one-to-one letter-sound correspondences.			✓		✓
ELA-LITERACY.RF.K.3.C	Read common high-frequency words by sight.			✓		✓
MATH.K.OA.A.5	Fluently add and subtract within 5.			✓		✓
MATH.K.CC.B.4.A	When counting objects, say the number names in the standard order, pairing each object with one and only one number name and each number name with one and only one object.				✓	✓
MATH.K.OA.A.1	Represent addition and subtraction with objects, fingers, mental images, drawings, sounds (e.g., claps), acting out situations, verbal explanations, expressions, or equations.				✓	✓
MATH.K.NBT.A.1	Compose and decompose numbers from 11 to 19 into ten ones and some further ones, e.g., by using objects or drawings, and record each composition or decomposition by a drawing or equation (such as 18 = 10 + 8); understand that these numbers are composed of ten ones and one, two, three, four, five, six, seven, eight, or nine ones.				✓	✓

First Grade Common Core Standards

Standard	Description	Little Parts	Random Emoji	FAC	Math Reps	SKAT
ELA-LITERACY.L.1.1.B	Use common, proper, and possessive nouns.	✓				✓
ELA-LITERACY.L.1.1.F	Use frequently occurring adjectives.	✓				✓
ELA-LITERACY.L.1.1.J	Produce and expand complete simple and compound declarative, interrogative, imperative, and exclamatory sentences in response to prompts.	✓				✓
ELA-LITERACY.L.1.2	Demonstrate command of the conventions of standard English capitalization, punctuation, and spelling when writing.		✓			✓
ELA-LITERACY.W.1.3	Write narratives in which they recount two or more appropriately sequenced events, include some details regarding what happened, use temporal words to signal event order, and provide some sense of closure.		✓			✓
ELA-LITERACY.SL.1.6	Produce complete sentences when appropriate to task and situation.		✓			✓
ELA-RF.1.3	Know and apply grade-level phonics and word analysis skills in decoding words.			✓		✓
MATH.1.OA.C.6	Add and subtract within 20			✓		✓
MATH.1.NBT.C.5	Given a two-digit number, mentally find 10 more or 10 less than the number, without having to count; explain the reasoning used.			✓		✓
MATH.1.NBT.B.2	Understand that the two digits of a two-digit number represent amounts of tens and ones. Understand the following as a special cases.				✓	✓
MATH.1.NBT.C.5	Given a two-digit number, mentally find 10 more or 10 less than the number, without having to count; explain the reasoning used.				✓	✓
MATH.1.OA.C.5	Relate counting to addition and subtraction (e.g., by counting on 2 to add 2).				✓	✓

Second Grade Common Core Standards

Standard	Description	Little Parts	Random Emoji	FAC	Math Reps	SKAT
ELA-LITERACY.L.2.1.E	Use adjectives and adverbs, and choose between them depending on what is to be modified.	✓				✓
ELA-LITERACY.L.2.1.F	Produce, expand, and rearrange complete simple and compound sentences (e.g., The boy watched the movie; The little boy watched the movie; The action movie was watched by the little boy).	✓				✓
ELA-LITERACY.L.2.1.B	Form and use frequently occurring irregular plural nouns (e.g., feet, children, teeth, mice, fish).	✓				✓
ELA-LITERACY.W.2.3	Write narratives in which they recount a well-elaborated event or short sequence of events, include details to describe actions, thoughts, and feelings, use temporal words to signal event order, and provide a sense of closure.		✓			✓
ELA-LITERACY.L.2.2	Demonstrate command of the conventions of standard English capitalization, punctuation, and spelling when writing.		✓			✓
ELA-LITERACY.L.2.1	Demonstrate command of the conventions of standard English grammar and usage when writing or speaking.		✓			✓
ELA-LITERACY.L.2.4.C	Use a known root word as a clue to the meaning of an unknown word with the same root			✓		✓
MATH.2.OA.B.2	Fluently add and subtract within 20 using mental strategies. By end of Grade 2, know from memory all sums of two one-digit numbers.			✓		✓
MATH.2.NBT.B.5	Fluently add and subtract within 100 using strategies based on place value, properties of operations, and/or the relationship between addition and subtraction. Fluently add and subtract within 20			✓		✓
MATH.2.NBT.A.1	Understand that the three digits of a three-digit number represent amounts of hundreds, tens, and ones; e.g., 706 equals 7 hundreds, 0 tens, and 6 ones. Understand the following as special cases:				✓	✓
MATH.2.NBT.A.3	Read and write numbers to 1000 using base-ten numerals, number names, and expanded form.				✓	✓
MATH.2.MD.C.7	Tell and write time from analog and digital clocks to the nearest five minutes, using a.m. and p.m.				✓	✓

Throughout this book, you will also find QR codes that link to resources, templates, and student work that will help to further explain the EduProtocols, Smart Start, and other resources. We've broken the book into four sections:

1. Introduction: Explains what EduProtocols are and why you should use them.
2. Smart Start: Lays out everything you need in order to set students up for success by helping them learn to learn.
3. EduProtocols: Describes five EduProtocols that have been redesigned specifically for the primary classroom.
4. Smart Start EduProtocols: Provides three more remixes of EduProtocols that will help you to make the most of Smart Start.

Don't worry if you need more support. EduProtocols are all about #oversharing. We are just a post or message away. As you have questions, you can connect with us on various social media platforms, including EduProtocols Plus. We love to answer questions and can guide you through your EduProtocol adoption process.

Ben & Jenn

Find us on X: @Techy_Jenn or @cogswell_ben!

Marlena & Jon

Find us on X: @jcorippo and @mhebern and at @eduprotocols!

A Note on Font Choice and Readability for Students

The font we chose to use in this book is called Lexend. Lexend was created by educational therapist Bonnie Shaver-Troup, EdD, in 2000. Lexend came about from a desire to make reading easier for everyone, and we've fallen in love with it, especially for our primary students! To learn more about Lexend, visit Dr. Shaver-Troup's website at www.lexend.com.

Learn more about Lexend.

lexend.com

Chapter 2
Why EduProtocols?

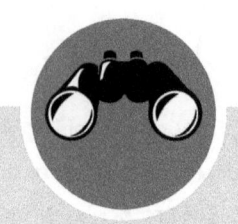

> **Jon**
>
> When we do different tasks each day, it adds an invisible, constant cognitive demand on students. Some (like me in 1969 in kindergarten) get overwhelmed and seem lost. They may act out or never complete tasks. With EduProtocols, students get more confident each day because they know what a completed EduProtocol looks like.

> **Marlena**
>
> For students with special needs, or our English language learners, the consistency that EduProtocols provide is especially reassuring.

In chapter 1, we broadly discussed the benefits of EduProtocols as "frames" that can be wrapped around any class content. But what particular need do EduProtocols meet, and how do we know they are effective from a learning and development perspective?

Principally, EduProtocols are designed to make the most of students' capacities in classroom learning. When students jump from one activity to the next, day in and day out, they lose their ability to focus on the content. That perpetual relearning of tasks wears on students, especially on primary students, who are still developing confidence at school. The EduProtocols allow students to learn one task and then apply it to a variety of content lessons, thus maximizing their energy and focusing their effort on the content at hand.

In this way, EduProtocols capitalize on what we know about how to optimize student learning. The zone of proximal development (ZPD) was theorized by Lev Vygotsky in the 1930s and describes a state of mind when a learner is working in the space between "cannot complete on my own" (frustration) and "can completely do on my own" (boredom). Too much, too fast, and the learner shuts down. Too slow, and the learner does not pay close attention because they already know it all. Just right, and the learner excels with confidence. When students work in the space between cannot and can, they are challenged at just the right level and are most open to new learning.

Managing the cognitive load, the ZPD of the student experience, is the magic dust of the EduProtocols that makes all the other goodness possible. By scaffolding learning with the EduProtocols, we allow the ZPD to become hyperfocused on content instead of lesson design. Students, regardless of age, feel enormously successful when they accomplish a lesson with little direction because they already know how.

How Learning an EduProtocol Is Like an Instagram Post

If you are trying to wrap your brain around the EduProtocols concept, it might be helpful to think about the process of posting on Instagram. There are several specific steps to sharing an image:

1. Find the perfect shot.
2. Take a photo.
3. Open the app.
4. Add the image to the app.
5. Edit the image.
6. Write your caption, tag people in your post, and include hashtags.
7. Wait for your friends to see your picture and comment.
8. The next time, you might try a filter. Here comes the creativity!

Can you see how the ZPD will shift in the Instagram example? At first, it's all about posting, but later it becomes about the artistry of the image. The next time you find that perfect shot, you will repeat the same basic steps to post the image. Those steps remain the same, but the image changes each time you post.

Could you imagine, by contrast, how frustrating it would be if the steps required to post an image on Instagram changed every time we tried to share a photo? That frustration is what happens when we consistently change the structure for content delivery and assessment in the TK–2 classroom. By keeping learning structures relatively similar—using the frames of EduProtocols—we help students focus on what really matters: learning new curricular content.

Using Instagram feels complicated at first. It is a struggle to make just the right edits. However, with a little practice, the process becomes familiar, and you soon find that your concentration shifts to the art of framing the perfect composition instead of how to find the photo library in the app.

Students will do the same with EduProtocols. Once they grow into them, they will shift their focus from the logistics of the lesson procedures to the art and joy of actual learning, a key strategy when content difficulty increases as students move through the year. With the slightly gamified approach of EduProtocols, students are often willing to tackle work beyond their initial abilities.

The Importance of Reps

It takes most classes two to five repetitions of an EduProtocol to master it. With primary students, it may take a little longer, as they may also be learning to use technology for the first time even as they are learning the EduProtocol. The sweet spot for an EduProtocol is when automaticity is reached, and the student's focus shifts from how to complete the process of the protocol to mastering the content that it frames. You'll know when this happens because you will be able to feel it in the classroom: students will recognize the EduProtocol by name and get right to work completing it.

Experienced teachers understand the importance of training students in the first days of school in face-to-face classrooms, and the most successful teachers take time in the first weeks of school to develop classroom procedures: where to get paper, when to sharpen pencils, how to put away laptops, and how to exit the classroom. Early training with EduProtocols will give you a head start in deploying EduProtocols in your classroom. We call this important first process Smart Start.

Smart Start is the method of introducing an EduProtocol to students with fun, light, and simple content. But if you are starting late in the year, or introducing an EduProtocol midway through the year, simply take time to allow students to learn the process before diving into your content. Go slow to go fast. You will reap the benefits later, and your time up front will pay off.

If you're new to Smart Start, don't worry. We'll provide a complete guide to conducting Smart Start in chapters 4 through 7. Then, once we've explored five major EduProtocols in section 3, we'll explain how to tailor them specifically for Smart Start in chapters 14 through 16.

Embracing the Four Cs with EduProtocols

EduProtocols are valuable in part because they seamlessly saturate classroom learning in a set of learning skills called the Four Cs. There has been buzz around the Four Cs for the last several years. The reason behind the buzz is that the Four Cs are vital for student learning and, more importantly, high-quality classroom engagement. Much research has been done to prove why the Four Cs are essential in life, but we think they are important because they motivate students to be critical thinkers, allow for creative expression, and teach students how to communicate with others and how to work together toward a common goal. When companies hire, they often look for these skills in order to compete in a twenty-first-century workforce. Also, as educators, we can see how these skills are essential for helping students become well-rounded individuals, and EduProtocols makes integrating the Four Cs that much easier.

Not familiar with the Four Cs or wondering why they apply to primary learners? The Four Cs are communication, critical thinking, creativity, and collaboration. Many articles about the Four Cs describe these skills as necessary for students to be successful in the modern workplace, and the Four Cs are cornerstones to a successful academically oriented classroom. This is because all people, including our primary learners, need to know how to communicate; what it looks like to collaborate, take turns, and learn from each other; how to problem solve when faced with challenges; and that there is not one right way to do things. Creativity also allows our students

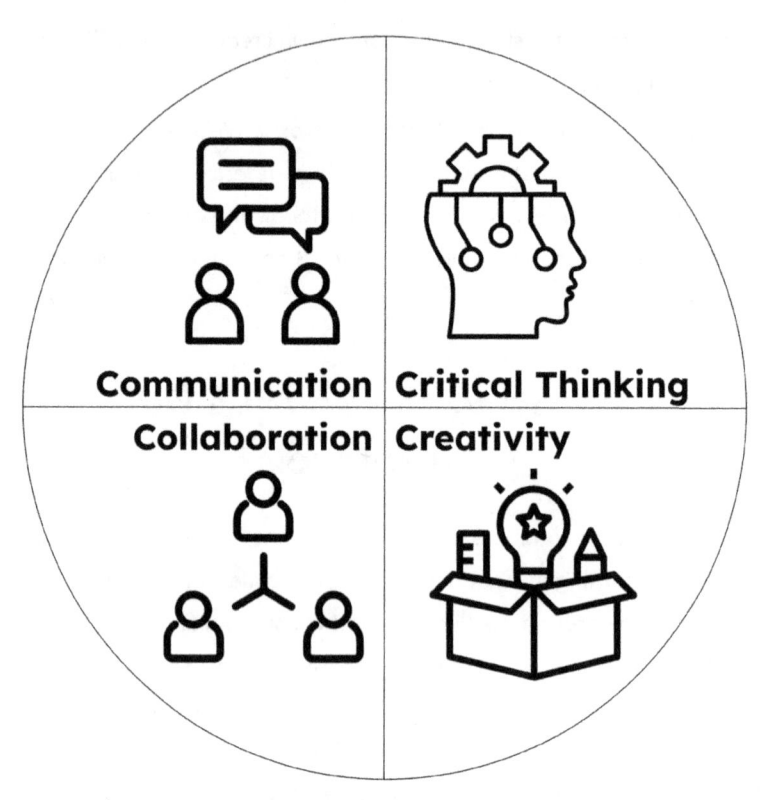

The Four Cs

> **Marlena**
>
> The Four Cs are called "soft skills" because they are the skills that any employer will look for in a candidate, and they are developed over a lifetime of learning!

a creative outlet, which is essential for social and emotional learning (SEL).

Here is a quick explanation of each of the Four Cs in our own words. (Whole books and numerous articles have been written on the Four Cs if you're eager to learn more.)

- **Communication**: Talking or sharing information with each other. This can be done face-to-face or asynchronously.
- **Critical Thinking:** Analyzing and/or thinking through a concept, issue, or idea. This goes beyond the easy answers and seeks deeper thought and evaluation.
- **Collaboration:** Working together to complete a task or project. This can be done in pairs, small groups, or as a whole class. Typically, students need to communicate in order to collaborate.
- **Creativity:** Engaging the imagination or nonstandard thinking in ways that can produce new and original ideas.

EduProtocols are dripping with Four Cs–rich learning. While some of the EduProtocols contain all the Four Cs, most contain at least two or three of them. We like to build in Four Cs-based tasks from day one so that student learning is authentic and engaging. The more students are engaged in their learning, the more they learn. Simple!

3, 2, 1, Blast Off!

Now it's time to blast off into the heart of the book. So curl up in a comfy chair and grab your beverage of choice, some note-taking devices, and whatever else you may need to begin your journey into EduProtocols for the primary classroom.

> **Jon**
> In EduProtocols, our goal is to design activities that have two or three of the Four Cs every time. It's not a "one C at a time" game. You don't have to add Four Cs to an EduProtocol—they are already built in.

> **Marlena**
> A Universal Design for Learning-friendly format means that the EduProtocols, by their open-response nature, easily adapt to a variety of learner abilities. But let's not get ahead of ourselves. Ben and Jenn will cover all of that in the pages to come!

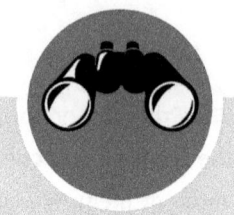

Chapter 3
Why Seesaw?

EduProtocols can be done using any platform, such as Microsoft, Google Workspace, or Canva. They can also be done in a wide variety of programs, such as Nearpod or Pear Deck. And they can also be done on paper. In fact, in our own classrooms, we really emphasize a balance of tech and paper for primary students. However, when we are going to use tech, we love Seesaw. In many sections of this book, you are going to see a part that says, "How It Looks in Seesaw." If you don't already use Seesaw, that's okay; we will also explain how to evaluate if a technology platform is compatible with an EduProtocol.

What Is Seesaw?

Seesaw is a learning platform, just like Google Classroom or ClassDojo, that's usable on any device and that allows students to demonstrate their learning in a variety of ways. Seesaw's website describes it as "a platform for student engagement. Teachers can empower students to create, reflect, share, and collaborate. Students 'show what they know' using photos, videos, drawings, text, PDFs, and links."

These tools are all built directly into Seesaw, making it very accessible to all students. Want your students to take a daily picture of their plants growing for their science journal? Seesaw can do that! Want them to record their weekly fluency passage? Seesaw can do that! Want them to practice symmetry with shape pattern blocks? Seesaw can do that! Everything is built directly into this simple platform.

Not only does Seesaw have amazing tools for your students to show what they know, it also has a built-in activity library. The activity library is filled with thousands of activities for TK–2 learners, including our own EduProtocols activities. These activities are already made, and all you have to do is assign them to your students. Additionally, it has an amazing built-in messaging feature that allows you to message families, send out newsletters, and so much more. Therefore, it is not only a platform for the students and teachers but also families, making it a true one-stop-shop kind of platform for our primary classrooms. You can scan the QR code to learn more about Seesaw.

> Watch to learn more about using Seesaw.
>
> tinyurl.com/whyseesawEP

Why Do We Love Seesaw?

You can do any EduProtocol in any way, but when you add it to Seesaw and use that microphone and recording feature, it comes alive. We *love* the Seesaw microphone! With it, students are able to add their own voice, by recording it, to any EduProtocol they do, which not only makes the protocol livelier but also helps students build language. The more we can get students to talk about what they are learning, the more they learn. Also, by using the microphone, students are essentially repeating a part of the rep, getting more practice with the content, and explaining their learning in another way.

There's much more to Seesaw than just the microphone. One of the EduProtocols we use a lot is Sketch and Tell. When we think of TK–2 students sketching using a digital platform, we cannot think of a platform better than Seesaw. Why? Because of the tools and simplicity of drawing digitally. Seesaw has numerous pen options, and teaching our younger learners how to use them is much easier than other platforms we have used. Also, students can still sketch on paper but take a picture of their sketch on Seesaw. Then they can use different tools for the tell side. Do they want to do a video, type a response, or record their voice for a response? The options are vast, which allows students to have more choice and creativity in their work.

Want to learn more about why we love Seesaw and all the amazing things you can do with it? Visit the extended content section of our website to get the whole enchilada!

> **Jon**
>
> As our friend Sam Patterson said: "Don't raise your hand, I'm calling on everyone." Tools like Seesaw allow educators to stop using popsicle sticks and other demeaning ways to see student work. You can see everyone right away and coach and grow them so much faster with edtech tools!

> **Marlena**
>
> Sketch and Tell is a protocol where students sketch a concept and then retell it to a partner before drawing in Seesaw, creating a powerful visualization protocol for students!

> **Extended Content:**
> Why We ♥ Seesaw!
>
> **We love Seesaw** for a ton of reasons. You may already love Seesaw as well. If you are not familiar with Seesaw, here are several more reasons why we prefer Seesaw as our tool of choice.
>
> Here are just some of the reasons why we love Seesaw!
> ★ The drawing and recording tools
> ★ Backgrounds and manipulatives
> ★ The Seesaw Activity Library
> ★ Parent communication features
> ★ Options to embed multiple medias
> ★ Simplicity of use
>
> tinyurl.com/WeLoveSeesaw
> Password: 73468

Finding the Perfect Learning Platform

We could go on and on about why we love Seesaw, but maybe you still are not convinced, or you have another platform you really love. That's okay! If you aren't ready, or don't want to use Seesaw, you don't have to. There are lots of other platforms that work great with EduProtocols for TK–2 students.

How do you know if the platform is right for EduProtocols? We look for apps that provide ways students can show their thinking, such as taking a picture and recording voice on top of it (awesome for read-overs), or taking a picture and recording and drawing on the canvas. One of our biggest priorities is that we want students to be able to record. We love a tool that lets teachers *and* students record.

We also look for a platform that gives students a voice in their choices. This means that students have options for showing what they know. Though it's possible to use several different platforms to show thinking in different ways, it can take a long time for students to learn the different tools, which is another reason we like Seesaw.

Another key feature we look for in a platform is accessibility and ease of use. When you are evaluating a tool, start by counting the amount of clicks needed in order for students to perform a particular task. We prefer apps that are easy for students to navigate with user-friendly tools. Ideally, platforms should use icons instead of just text. If a teacher can add video or audio instructions to a technology tool, then this is also super helpful for providing immediate guidance without relying on the UI itself. Some tools have a "read to me" feature, which can be very helpful if you can record video or audio instructions.

Learning platforms also need to be broadly and immediately available. Students should be able to access a tool easily. Ideally, login should be facilitated by a centralized Google or Microsoft account, and apps should be accessible through a school or district portal. If students can't access a tool quickly, or if students need to hop between several apps in order to complete activities, you may want to think twice about using a given technology tool, as it is likely to suck away important instructional time. To that end, another key feature we look for in a platform is an activity library where we can store our templates and reuse them over and over again, so that they can help to maximize the time-saving nature of EduProtocols.

> **Jon**
>
> The EduProtocols aren't dependent on platforms or apps. EduProtocols are pedagogical strategies that will still be effective no matter what tech kids have. It's still all about MathReps, Sketch and Tell, or Little p*ARTS.

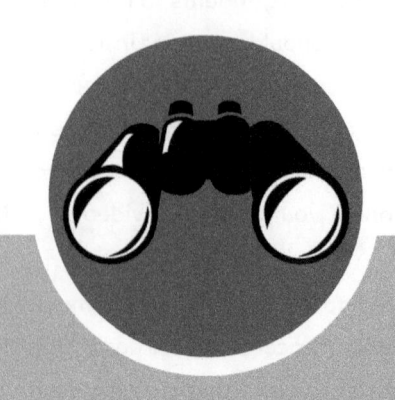

SECTION 2
Smart Start

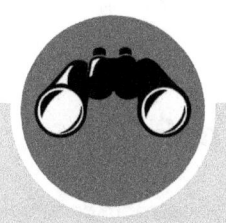

Chapter 4
Building Culture

The most beautiful things in the world cannot be seen or touched, they are felt with the heart.
—Antoine de Saint-Exupéry, *The Little Prince*

As EduProtocols creators Marlena Hebern and Jon Corippo say in *The EduProtocol Field Guide, Book 1*, "Culture is everything." We agree.

Establishing an effective culture from day one creates a smooth rest of the year. We want kids to be excited to come to school and engage in their learning. We can describe classrooms that run smoothly, that build routines, and that establish a positive vibe as having a positive classroom culture. In these classrooms, students contribute throughout and feel good about their experiences. Regardless of how seamless it looks, building a positive culture takes time, persistence, and patience. Our goal as teachers should not be to create a classroom of quiet compliance, but rather a place of exciting engagement and positivity.

> **Marlena**
>
> Building culture allows us to set the stage for the work of EduProtocols. It's hard for students to work together when a classroom lacks respect and cohesiveness. So we begin to establish this very early in the process.

Extended Content:
Smart Start: Building Culture

Building culture is an integral part of making sure your class is successful throughout the year. In this section, we will expand on some ways to help ensure the success of EduProtocols.

In the extended content, you'll get:
- ★ Making mistakes as an essential part of the learning process
- ★ Building classroom essential agreements
- ★ Making class movies to establish routines
- ★ Creating class graphs with emojis from Things That Rock
- ★ Using classroom jobs to build community
- ★ Design Thinking tips and challenges

tinyurl.com/ssbuildingculture
Password: 73468

What's in a Name?

A HUGE part of building culture is building the classroom community. So often, we as teachers get right into teaching our routines and getting into the year without taking the time needed to build that classroom community.

This is especially true when it comes to names. Knowing your classmates by name is one way to help establish this desired classroom culture. Students may have classroom jobs, and know they have friends in the classroom, but do they know the names of each and every classmate?

Although it seems like it should be easy for students to learn their classmates' names, we always find it takes a while. That is why one of our goals in building culture is getting students to learn each other's names as soon as possible, so that when students start working on EduProtocols, they feel more connected to their peers when engaged in the work of EduProtocols.

Helping students learn each other's names can easily hook into other beginning-of-the-year rituals. For example, first-day pictures seem to be a staple at many schools. We can use these pictures for more than classroom decoration. Students love seeing themselves, and their peers, on the screen, so try creating a slideshow of these student pictures and play it as students enter the room each day. If you can add a typed name to students' pictures, even better.

You can also use this slideshow as your morning greeting. When a student picture comes up, have the class say, for example, "Good morning, Stella." This gives every student a chance to be seen and heard from the beginning of the day. As an alternative or extension, put the students' names in a random name selector and run through the names in the morning. When a student's name comes up, we can say good morning as a group.

Another great name-learning activity involves printing out students' pictures and passing them out to the class. Working in pairs, students can hold up another student's picture and ask what the student's name is. This activity not only helps students practice each other's names but also builds Partner Talk.

Ben

One of the first questions I ask my own kids when they come home from school right after the school year starts is, "Did you make any new friends or meet any new people?" Oftentimes, my children will say yes, but when I ask their friend's name, they often shrug and look at me blankly.

Ben & Jenn

So often students would just point to tell me, "He is doing a good job." When I would say, "What is his name?" they would respond, "I don't know." This told me we need to really focus on names, and hey, there is an EduProtocol for that!

Jon

True story: In November of my first-grade year, kids called me Short Stuff. My teacher said, "Call him by his name, boys." They shrugged and said, "We don't know his name." This is part of why I'm passionate about Smart Start. As educators, we need to create classrooms where this doesn't happen.

Welcome Christopher

🚀 Be Kind 🚀 Be Safe 🚀 Be Your Best 🚀

Create welcome slides from the first-day photos!

Students might not learn all their friends' names by the end of the first day, but hopefully they will do so as soon as possible. Keep practicing names every day, and your classroom culture and identity will begin to take shape.

Class-Building with Smart Start

As educators, we know how important the first six weeks of school are. As primary educators, this time is even more important because kids are still learning how to do school. This is an essential time to create a culture where students feel safe, welcome, and excited about learning. It is also a time to establish routines, get to know students, and create a community of engaged learners and kind humans. Smart Start is a way to build this while also preparing students for mastering academic standards using EduProtocols. It is a way to start your classroom smarter by working on creating this beautiful classroom culture while also getting right into the work.

Things That Rock: Would You Rather

One of our favorite ways to establish classroom culture is by playing games like Things That Rock in a "Would You Rather" format. With Things That Rock, students simply look at one thing, such as going

Ben & Jenn

To amp it up a bit, run Fast and Curious (chapter 10) or Sketch and Tell (chapter 12) as name-learning activities.

Jon

Smart Start makes the first weeks of school smooth by making procedures *and* classwork become second nature. By the end, all the kids will know each other. There's plenty of time to get to know them yourself afterward.

Ben & Jenn

Here are some easy-to-run classroom activities that will help you to implement Smart Start and establish an ideal classroom culture while building toward competency with several EduProtocols.

Ben & Jenn

We love getting students speaking in complete sentences as soon as possible. It takes time, but it is so helpful to students' academic development.

Jenn's Would You Rather Slide Deck

tinyurl.com/jennwyrather

Marlena

Using sentence stems with week one or two vocabulary and sight words is a fun way to help front-load younger students on what is to come.

Ben & Jenn

This activity also leads right into introducing students to the Little Random Emoji Writing EduProtocol (chapter 9). Some examples begin with pulling up two random emojis. Students draw or write which one is their favorite, or pick one and tell something they like about it. They can start working on opinion sentences and so much more.

to the beach for a day, and they place themselves on a continuum to tell if going to the beach rocks or does not rock. In Would You Rather, students look at two things, like going to the beach or going to a water park, and they decide which rocks more.

You can use emojis to play this game as a way to introduce students to the Little Random Emoji Writing EduProtocol (chapter 9). Have two emojis on the screen with the question. You can practice routines like whole-class reading and pointing to the words as you read while also letting the students get to know each other.

This activity is great for so many reasons. First, students start making connections with each other because they notice that some peers like the same thing. It also gives us an idea of what topics and ideas engage the class. Second, it's fun, and students' endorphins start kicking in, helping make a positive impression of school.

As a bonus, this game builds academic skills. This game is a great opportunity to model the importance of answering in complete sentences. One thing we notice is students will often just answer "Cheeseburger" or "Pizza" when asked, for example, which foods they prefer. Use this exercise to teach conversations and talking in sentences. So, instead of saying "Pizza," students are directed to respond with "I would rather have pizza." This is a more organic way to get students learning those effective communication strategies as well as practicing speaking and listening/language standards (SL K.6 SL 1.6, SL 2.6, L L K.1, L 1.1, L 2.1).

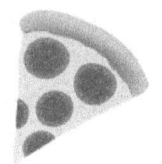

Would you rather have a cheeseburger or a slice of pizza?

Would You Rather Smart Start is a fun way to get to know your students.

The more you play this game, the more practice students get with speaking and listening, and they get to know each other. For a whole slide deck of Would You Rather slides, visit tinyurl.com/jennwyrather or tinyurl.com/BensWYR.

> Use the EduProtocols Random Emoji Generator to randomly generate two emojis for Would You Rather at eduprotocols.com/class.
>
> tinyurl.com/BensWYR

Use the EduProtocols Random Emoji Generator to randomly generate two emojis for Would You Rather.

Would You Rather with Sticky Notes

As much as we love Would You Rather, it can be challenging at the beginning of the year for some of our younger students. Let's take the slide with the pizza and the cheeseburger. "Okay, kindergarten students! We are going to choose between pizza and a cheeseburger," we tell them. "Remember," we caution, "you can only stand up once and choose one or the other. Stand up if you would rather have pizza." Most of the class stands up. "Now," we insist, "stand up if you would rather have a cheeseburger." Most of the class stands up again.

If you teach younger students, you may have seen this phenomenon before. We call it the "Everyone Picks Everything" phenomenon. Kids either don't know which to pick, watch what their classmates pick, or just aren't sure what to do. So how do we get kids to choose one option or the other? A simple sticky note can solve this problem.

Marlena
Have students physically move to one end of the room or the other. If they cannot decide, they can position themselves in the middle!

Ben
It can be helpful to do a quick model drawing of each image at the beginning of the year. Also, you can consider having students write the word under the drawing.

> **Ben & Jenn**
>
> This Would You Rather Post-it note activity is a great way to start with Sketch and Tell.

> **Jon**
>
> Remember what Sam Patterson said: "Don't raise your hand, I'm calling on everyone." Better design and edtech can keep educators from "scaring kids into answering."

> **Ben & Jenn**
>
> Partner Talk is important in the classroom, but it is especially important for EduProtocols. Students need this practice regularly, not only for EduProtocols but to build the language they need to be academically successful.

> **Ben**
>
> As an instructional coach, I went into a lot of classrooms. One thing I noticed was that students were fairly good at asking questions but not the greatest at answering them.

Here's how to run this variation of Would You Rather:

1. Once you review the choices for a given Would You Rather question, hand out sticky notes.
2. Have students go back to their seats and quickly sketch the item they would prefer.
3. Direct students to come back to the carpet and share which item they chose. They also have a scaffold to refer to if you first have them share their sketches with a partner.
4. Once students understand the game, you can start making simple class graphs of responses. Or, for a more active option, line students up by choice as a nice lead-in to creating class graphs.

Partner Talk

Popsicle sticks with students' names are often used to get students to answer questions. This is something we see in classrooms all over as a way to help encourage all students to answer questions. Although this may increase participation, does it really get more students participating?

Partner Talk is an effective strategy to engage 100 percent of students. Also called "Think-Pair-Share," this strategy is heavily used in TK–2 classrooms and can be highly effective. What happens, though, when students partner up but have no idea what to do? We need to teach students how to talk to each other in order for strategies like Partner Talk to be effective.

Teaching Partner Talk with *Brown Bear, Brown Bear, What Do You See?* Cards

"Brown Bear, Brown Bear what do you see? I see a ___ ___ looking at me."

If you are a TK–2 teacher, or parent, you can possibly recite much of Bill Martin Jr.'s book *Brown Bear, Brown Bear, What Do You See?* by memory. This is a traditional pattern book, which can get kids into reading. However, we like to use this book to encourage students to talk with partners.

One of the reasons we love *Brown Bear, Brown Bear, What Do You See?* is it has a question-and-answer pattern. We use this pattern to get students into asking and answering questions in a short period of time.

Here's how to run *Brown Bear, Brown Bear, What Do You See?* as a Partner Talk primer:

1. Prepare 1–3 sets of colored animal cards of the animals that are in the book: a brown bear, a purple cat, a white dog, etc. You need at least one card of each animal featured in the book, and you need enough cards for each student to have one.

2. Read the book for a few days so students get the question-and-answer pattern as well as the animals and colors. Students don't need to know the order of the book, but the animal and color vocabulary is important and keeps students interested in the content for a longer period of time.

3. Model the Partner Talk. First, we explain that the goal of this activity is to learn how to ask and answer questions in complete sentences. Then, select one student to come up, and you each hold up a card in front of you so that the other person can see it. From there, one person asks, "What do you see?" while the other person answers, "I see a ____ _____ looking at me." Bam. Both partners have shared in this easy structure.

4. After a few students model the activity with you, have them come up and model it with each other.

Once students are comfortable with this activity, they are ready for the next one.

Ben

It may seem silly, but you really need to teach students how to hold the card so that the other partner can see it. As a non-example, I model holding it backward and upside down.

Ben

English language learners pick up this activity relatively quickly. I really like using this structure because even my students who have never spoken English before are successful.

Jenn

Other fun books to do this with are *If You Give a Mouse a Cookie*, *If You Give a Moose a Muffin*, or other books from that series. Think about integrating a letter of the week. For example, if the class is learning about the letter *D*, read *If You Give a Dog a Donut* and do this activity to practice Partner Talk.

Colored Bracelets with Dots on the Floor

> **Ben**
>
> Some people will call this structure "lines of communication."

This activity offers major scaffolding for students to get better at Partner Talk.

Please note that this can be done in a few different ways, but we use colored dots, or sit spots, and two different colored bracelets. The dots help students know where to stand, and the bracelets tell students whose turn it is.

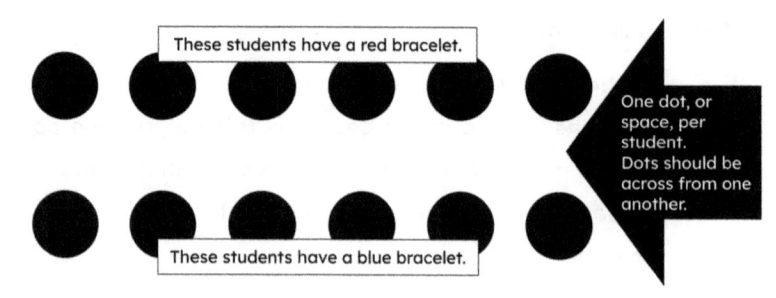

> **Ben**
>
> I also use this time to build community. Students greet each other with a high five and by name. Students also do the same and say thank you before they move on to the next partner.

These students have a red bracelet.

One dot, or space, per student. Dots should be across from one another.

These students have a blue bracelet.

Stage students for Partner Talk.

1. Set the dots on the floor in two parallel lines. There should be enough dots for all students.
2. Direct students to face each other, with calm bodies, and make eye contact.
3. Pass out bracelets. Each line gets a different colored bracelet. For example, one line gets a red bracelet, while the other line gets a blue bracelet.
4. Tell students which color bracelet indicates that a group should go first, and make sure students know which bracelet they have.
5. Hand out the *Brown Bear* cards to all students. Review how to hold them and stand nicely.
6. Ask the first group of students to ask their partners, "What do you see?".
7. Direct the second group of students to respond in a complete sentence that begins with "I see."

> **Jenn**
>
> I find it very helpful to practice answering in a complete sentence. In this example, we would model and say, "I see a brown bear" instead of just saying, "Brown bear."

8. Instruct students to switch roles and repeat the process of asking, "What do you see?" and answering with a sentence that begins "I see."
9. When both groups have gone, ask students to indicate they are ready to move on.
10. After a round of asking and answering questions, switch partners. Everyone in one line slides one space over, and now they have a new partner. The last person in that line goes back to the other end of the line. Keep in mind that only one line moves while the other line stays put.

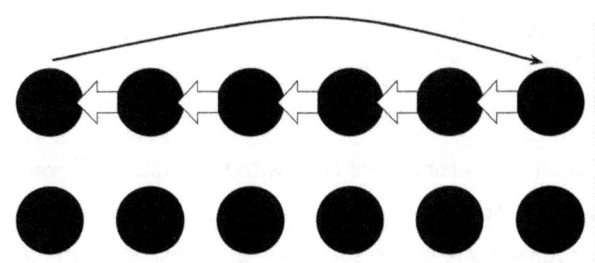

In only one line, the first person in the line goes to the back, and everyone slides down. If this is done correctly everyone should now have a new partner.

Rotate students in Partner Talk.

Practice this sequence for a few days with the *Brown Bear* cards, and then switch up the type of cards students have. For example, each student could get a card with a letter or number on it. The great part is students simply follow the same pattern. One partner asks, "What do you see?" and the other partner answers, "I see a _____." Again, this structure is super helpful for your English language learners, who will be speaking in no time.

The next step is having students practice with partners on the carpet or at their tables. In the beginning, we still distribute the partner bracelets and review who has a red bracelet and who has a blue bracelet. Then we can change up the question and skip the cards, and students are already used to asking and answering questions in a complete sentence. By the end, students are experts on Partner Talk, and you can start asking more difficult questions.

> **Jenn**
> Once they learn the strategy, you can do this with anything. In first and second grade, I would do this same thing with students' names. For example, "Ben, who do you see?" and have Ben respond, "I see Jenn looking at me," and vice versa, to help students learn each other's names.

> **Ben**
> I also mix this in with the Would You Rather, and students can practice with their sticky notes.

> **Jenn**
> In first and second grade, you can do this with four rows and four different colors, which will help you have smaller groups because the students already know their colors and can take it to that next level.

Think-Pair-Share

Think-Pair-Share is a little different than Partner Talk, but once learned it is an effective strategy that is used with many EduProtocols. It allows students the opportunity to think before sharing, which increases participation because more students feel safe to share, as they were given time to think about the question and their answer. After students are given their think time, they pair up in a variety of ways, which gets students talking to more students. Students do not just talk to the same students every day but really get familiar with everyone in the classroom. These skills create the true classroom community we strive for.

Think

After posing a question or prompt, we start with thinking. This is one of the most important parts of the activity because students need time to think in order to be ready to share. When we ask students to share right away, they may just stare and have no idea what to do because they did not have time to think about their response. Therefore, giving them time to prepare is 100 percent necessary.

However, simply telling students to think of their response is not enough. We know that even when we tell students to think, there will be at least one who still does not have a response when it is time to pair and then share. We need to be explicit in how we teach the "think" part. This means telling students what you want them to think about.

Be sure to give students context for what they are thinking about. For example, let's say we are learning about three-dimensional shapes. Some students might have some prior knowledge of what three-dimensional shapes are, and others may not. To provide context, begin by showing students a ball and asking students to think about words they could use to describe the ball.

Students may come up with words like *round*, *circle*, *bounce*, or just *ball*. They can think about how they would describe the ball before they pair and share with a partner. However, later in the lesson,

---

Marlena

These strategies are the building blocks for the skills students will use for success with EduProtocols.

Ben & Jenn

Some students will have an answer right away, and others will need more time and prompting. Without enough think time, this is where the think part in this strategy often fails.

Jenn

Asking questions helps students think more. Asking them questions like how they might describe the ball, what the ball can do, etc. helps them to think about more options for sharing. Guiding questions are essential for context.

after they have been given some context, they can think about the name of the three-dimensional shape a ball is.

Another important aspect of the think part of this strategy is the amount of time given. You want to make sure you have 100 percent participation, and this means giving all students enough time while not giving so much time that other students will become bored. There are two helpful strategies for this.

1. Have students show you when they have their response. This way you know what percent of students have their answers and who needs a little more help/time without making them feel bad about it.
2. As students are showing you they have their response ready, encourage them to think of more possible responses. For example, if their response is *round*, they can use the time to think of even more words to describe the ball, like *circle* or maybe even *sphere*.

Pair

After students have been given time to think, the next step is to pair up. We have all seen those few students looking for a partner even though there is someone right in front of them also looking for a partner. That is because this is another skill that needs to be taught. How? Teach students how to:

- turn to the person next to them.
- make groups of three when necessary.

You can also incorporate other strategies for helping students form pairs or groups:

- Play music and have students walk around the room and freeze when the music stops to partner up.
- Have students go back to their tables and partner up with their shoulder partner, face partner, or across the way partner.
- Direct students to partner up with the person next to them, or in front/behind them, or diagonal from them on the car-

Ben

Depending on the question, sometimes I will have students who have an answer share with the whole class before they share with a partner. This allows some of my students who don't have an answer to borrow someone else's, and then everyone can share.

Jenn

I use a physical cue so students can show me that they have their response. For example, I might tell them to give me a thumbs-up on their chest so I can quickly assess who has their response without intimidating others who are still thinking.

Ben & Jenn

If you have an uneven number, teach your students to notice when someone doesn't have a partner, and have the whole class invite them to join.

pet. We come up with fun names like "Peanut Butter and Jelly Partner" (the person next to you), "Taco Burrito Partner" (the person in front of or behind you), or your diagonal partner. On the carpet, this is similar to table partners.

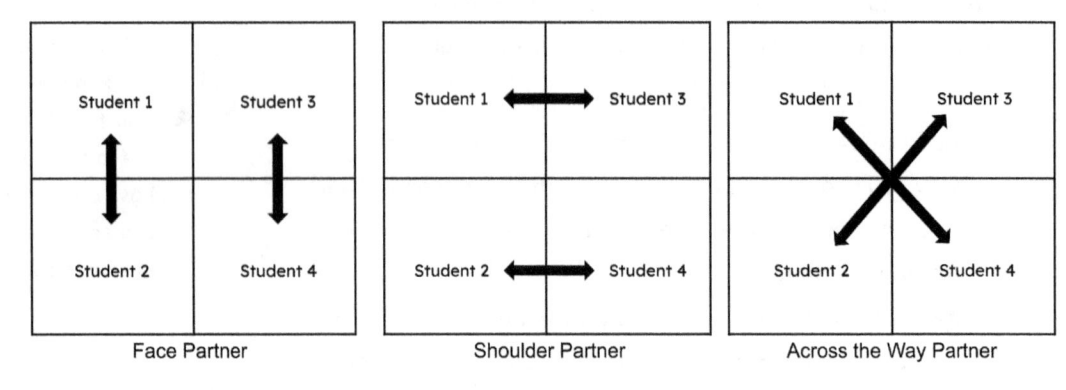

| Face Partner | Shoulder Partner | Across the Way Partner |

Types of pairings for table talk

> **Jenn** 
>
> If you have students mix and mingle with music, remind them not to just not to just follow their friends but walk around the room all over the place. When the music stops, they can high five or fist bump the person they are closest to. I like to have them say hello to their partner in any language they know or greet them by telling them it's nice to see them today before they share.

You can establish four dedicated "Clock" or "Season" partners with whom students will consistently pair up. This cuts down on the time needed for students to find partners and gives them variety as well.

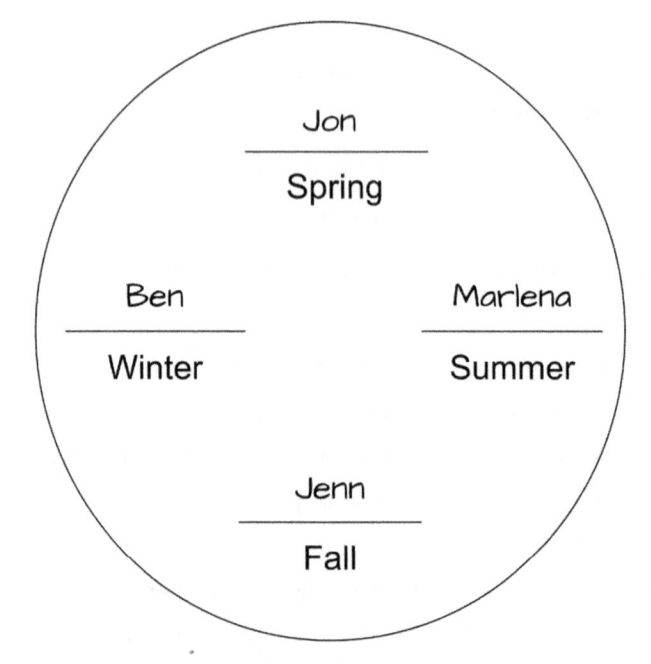

Jon — Spring
Ben — Winter
Marlena — Summer
Jenn — Fall

Example of Clock/Season partners

- Flippity.net is a great tool with which you can randomly assign partners in the classroom. The website is free and has a few different options as to how to input students. You can quickly pair up partners and change partners with the click of a button.

Using these strategies helps students quickly find a partner. We encourage varying your pair-up strategy, as students can become less engaged if you always use the same strategy.

Share

Once students have paired up, the next step is for them to share. One thing we notice is that students in the TK–2 classroom tend to just give their answers in single-word responses instead of sharing in complete sentences. For example, they may just say, "Round" instead of "The ball is round."

This can be changed by teaching how to share. One way we like to do this is by using a speaking frame. For example, we will write the speaking frame "The ball is _____" on the board and remind students to speak in a complete sentence.

At first, students' "frame" shares may seem a little robotic. However, the purpose is to model speaking in sentences, rather than telling students exactly how to speak. With practice, they learn to speak in their own sentences with less and less modeling.

Another thing we notice is that students do not always listen to each other. They get so caught up in their own share that they do not listen to their partners' share. One way to help this is to ask students, for example, "How did your partner describe the ball?" This way, students learn to listen more to what their partner says because that is what they will be sharing. By explicitly modeling and teaching how to Think-Pair-Share, you will get 100 percent participation and really see students learning.

Ben

I will usually just tell my kindergartners what the sentence frame could be and have them practice a few times with me. This keeps the flow going.

Ben

Consider just saying thank you when students share. That way, more students will be willing to share. You can always review the best answers after students share.

Directed Drawing

Every child is an artist, and every child's interpretation of the world is a masterpiece. However, if you have ever asked a young child to draw a representation of 3+2 and then painfully waited while they tried to draw a representation that ended up being completely unrecognizable, you know that sometimes it is helpful to front-load basic drawing skills with students so that they can more efficiently represent their ideas visually. For this, we can supplement our art instruction with Directed Drawing.

Directed Drawing is the process of showing students how to draw by breaking down an image into steps. Each student has their own drawing materials, and the teacher shows the drawing process for a given subject. Directed Drawing is an extremely modeled process in which the teacher shows the student exactly where to draw each line until the drawing is complete. Typically, we watch a video tutorial on a site like Art for Kids Hub (artforkidshub.com), then pause the video to model our own drawing as students also draw.

We know it's fun, but why do it? When our students walk into our classrooms, they are coming with a variety of experiences, knowledge, and backgrounds. As a result, not all students may understand how to draw a specific thing or where to even begin. Additionally, not all students may be comfortable with their ability to draw and color. In our classrooms, we want to create a culture where students feel safe and welcome, and where they all have opportunities to grow and learn. We want to provide students with the resources they need to be successful and gain confidence because confidence creates individuals who are not afraid to take risks, try new things, and learn from their mistakes. Utilizing the strategy of Directed Drawing helps students to be able to draw something they may have never heard of before and learn specific drawing skills that they can apply in future drawing experiences.

Directed Drawing also helps students learn to follow one- and two-step directions. In kindergarten and first grade, Directed Drawing should start one step at a time. As they get more practice, you

---

Jon

The Little Prince drew the scariest thing in the world: a brown blob that resembled the outline of a hat. The adults laughed. Is it a hat? Why is that scary? But it wasn't a hat at all! He had drawn a snake so powerful that it ate an elephant whole. Since adults were so simpleminded—they could not see the elephant inside the snake—he resolved to never draw for them again.

Ben

In the beginning, I will just do a Google search and find a step-by-step image of a Directed Drawing. I find these to be simpler, and students are more successful once they get the basics down.

Marlena

To ensure students have a creative voice in Directed Drawing, refer to the real object often (either an image or the actual object), and show students how to see and break down the parts of it into lines and shapes to create an image.

Ben & Jenn

One of our favorite EduProtocols is Sketch and Tell (chapter 12). However, when we think of our TK-2 students, we know that some students do not yet have the skills to sketch recognizable images. We can help prepare students for success by starting with Directed Drawing.

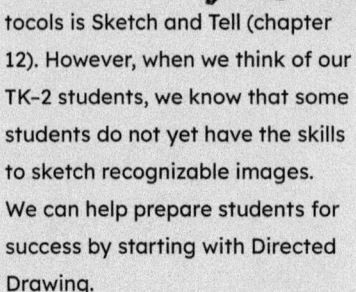

can start doing two steps at a time. In second grade, you can definitely start with two steps at a time and then work on three steps.

Directed Drawing Integrated with Writing and Speaking

If Directed Drawing helps students build a foundation for the Sketch part of Sketch and Tell, students can start building a foundation for the "tell" part by labeling their pictures. These labels can start as simply writing one word to tell about the picture (kindergarten) and then can build toward writing a full caption for their drawing (first and second grades). Not only can students label their pictures with writing, they can do this activity in Seesaw, hit the record button, and share all about their drawing by simply talking about it. This is a great way to start building digital fluency.

As students develop more skills, they can take their writing to the next level by writing a story, informational paragraph, opinion piece, or any type of writing to match their picture. For example, you could lead a Directed Drawing of a unicorn and a dragon and have the students write an opinion piece telling which creature is better with supporting reasons. Or you could do a Directed Drawing of a lighthouse, have students research different lighthouses, and instruct everyone to write paragraphs about lighthouses.

Ben

Not only does Directed Drawing help with sketching, but the skills can transfer over to handwriting.

Jenn

So that the Directed Drawings won't all look the same, I like to let students color them however they want. This starts to spark their creativity and lets them take something very modeled and make it their own. I'll also encourage them to add a background to the object we drew. For example, if we draw a unicorn, I might ask them where the unicorn lives or what our setting is going to be. This is a great way to encourage creativity and use academic language.

Ben

Sketching is integrated into lots of other EduProtocols beside Sketch and Tell. We do it in Emoji Writing, Thin Slides, MathReps, and sometimes Little p*ARTS.

Ben

They can also draw on paper, take a picture in Seesaw, and then share all about it.

Jenn

If students are not writing yet, they can still practice the "tell" part by showing their drawing to a partner and telling what they made. They can also tell a story, offer their opinion on what they have drawn, and so much more!

Ben

Adding details to a drawing is a jumping-off point to adding details to their writing.

Marlena

To balance Directed Drawing with creativity development in young children, be sure to layer in plenty of creative open-ended art experiences as explored in *Open-Ended Art for Young Children* by Tracy Galuski and Mary Ellen Bardsley. Or my absolute favorite go-to for creative primary art, *Scribble Art: Independent Process Art Experiences for Children* by MaryAnn F. Kohl.

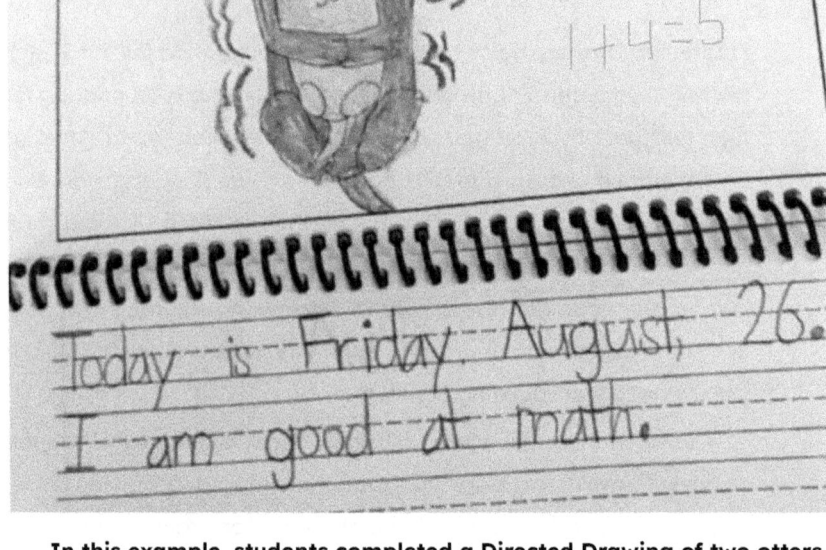

In this example, students completed a Directed Drawing of two otters.

Digital Directed Drawing

After students have developed their fine motor skills and the ability to follow two- and three-step directions on paper, they can learn how to do Digital Directed Drawings. The idea is that once students have learned the basics of Directed Drawing, you can build on their prior knowledge to teach them how to digitally draw. Teach Digital Directed Drawing the same way you teach it on paper. Use a video that is a Directed Drawing. Do each step at a time. As you do this, practice explaining what pen colors, size, and type you should use for each part. If they make a mistake, show them how to use the digital eraser or our favorite, the undo button. Oftentimes the undo button is better to use than the eraser. If you use the eraser, often you erase other parts of the drawing, whereas the undo button just removes the most recent change without interfering with the other parts of the drawing.

Imagine your students just created a beautiful digital drawing and accidentally erased something they did not mean to erase. They may continue to try and erase, causing the entire drawing to disappear. However, by showing them how to use the undo button, you've given them a way to be able to fix it and bring their drawing back to the way they intended it to be. If you had not shown them that, how frustrating would that have been for them? This is why it is so important to teach students to problem-solve, think critically, be creative, and communicate their thoughts and ideas.

Our favorite tool for Digital Directed Drawing is Seesaw because it:

- is extremely user-friendly.
- has multiple pen options.
- has built-in backgrounds, shapes, and more.
- allows students to change their colors easily.
- has an undo button, as well as an eraser.
- allows you to include the Directed Drawing as part of the activity so students can do it at their own pace.

The first few times you lead Digital Directed Drawing, you don't have to worry about adding any writing to it. If you are using Seesaw, just have students tap the microphone and record themselves telling about their picture a little. This will slowly introduce students to the skills necessary for the full Sketch and Tell EduProtocol.

Resources

YouTube is a great spot for Directed Drawing. Some recommended channels include:

- ArtHub for Kids: youtube.com/@artforkidshub
- Whimsy Workshop Teaching: tinyurl.com/whimworkteach
- Bilingual Scrapbook: youtube.com/@bilingualscrapbook9018
- One FAB Teacher: youtube.com/@OneFABTeacher

Ben

I like to create my own Digital Directed Drawing video and attach it to the Seesaw activity. That way, students can go back and watch it again if they want. Plus, the digital canvas has more dimensions than a piece of paper.

Jenn

Not all pens and pen sizes work for the Digital Directed Drawing. Teaching students how to pick which ones work for this purpose is a digital literacy skill they need.

Ben

When doing a Digital Directed Drawing, teach the students how to color the background first. Keep in mind when drawing digitally that you need to move from the back forward.

Jon

Ed Emberley books are spectacular for Directed Drawing beginners!

You can also just do a Google search like "directed drawing bear." Then you can click on images and find lots of different options for Directed Drawings.

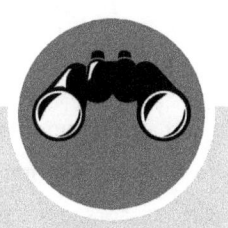

Chapter 5
Technology

Setting Students Up for Success

Using technology effectively can be a challenge at all ages or grade levels. It can be especially difficult for our youngest learners, who are still learning letters, numbers, and even how to use a computer.

With that being said, most, if not all, students come to the classroom with some basic understanding of how to use technology. If we set them up for success and support them along the way through Smart Start, teaching technology is no more difficult or challenging than teaching students how to use watercolor paints. Allowing for a lot of quick failure and letting kids learn iteratively is key. It is also important to understand that using technology is not optional anymore. Technology is not going away, and it is something that all students need to learn how to use in a balanced and effective way. Let's learn how to do that.

We will start off this chapter by giving some ideas on how to set students up for success. Some technological needs and concerns may be out of a teacher's control; however, a conversation with your principal or IT department head may, or may not, lead to changes. Sometimes if you plant a seed with an idea for change, it can come to fruition later. So don't give up, but be politely persistent.

We will start out this section with some extended content available online, and then we will move into some ideas on how to build trackpad and keyboarding skills.

> **Ben & Jenn**
> We know every teacher is at a different point with technology implementation. You may not need the tips in this chapter, but we wanted to make sure to start everyone off with success. Feel free to browse this chapter as you would like.

Remember, the goal of this chapter is to get your students to start using their devices with fluency. Just like we take the time to teach students to hold a pencil correctly, cut with scissors, and use a glue bottle, we need to make sure students can use their devices correctly and competently. We believe sometimes you can accomplish more with fewer apps. For us, starting with just a few apps or programs and building student skills to mastery maximizes learning time and really allows students to shine. Plus, once they learn one program well, many of those skills transfer over to other programs. Use Write the Room to support skills and enhance EduProtocols. Again, start with one thing. Repeat, repeat, repeat. Master it and introduce the next part. It is okay to start small to go big.

Extended Content:
Smart Start: Logging in & Device Care

Students caring for devices is one reason why teachers may be hesitant to use devices. In this section, we will share some tips to get students up and running with handling devices responsibly and safely.

In the extended content, you'll get:
- ★ Protocols for getting students to log in fluently and quickly
- ★ Tips to build routines for students and their devices
- ★ Tips for device care if students take home devices
- ★ Resources on how to train students for device care

tinyurl.com/ssdevicecare
Password: 73468

Trackpad Skills

Something as simple as using a trackpad can pose a challenge to students. We highly recommend touch screens for littles in general, but not all budgets can support one. If you are a teacher without a touch screen, then you must go over some trackpad basics.

Because they require fine motor skills, trackpads take time and patience for young students. Spending time teaching in the beginning can save a lot of time later. Regardless of grade level, it is good to take some time to review some of these skills. Modeling how to use a trackpad can be very helpful, and a great way to do this is putting your computer under a document camera.

We like to start by directing students to use one finger to move the mouse and click. Oftentimes, striking a balance between pushing too lightly and too hard poses a challenge for students. To address that issue, our first exercise involves having students gently rub their finger over the skin, simulating a moving mouse and then having them push down to click. We repeat moving and clicking together.

Teaching trackpad skills in context can be super helpful. Having students open Seesaw and practice drawing is a great lesson in cause and effect with the trackpad. Students quickly learn how they have to push down on the trackpad for the pen to work. If you haven't already noticed the theme, giving students time to play and draw in the beginning of the year can save a lot of time later.

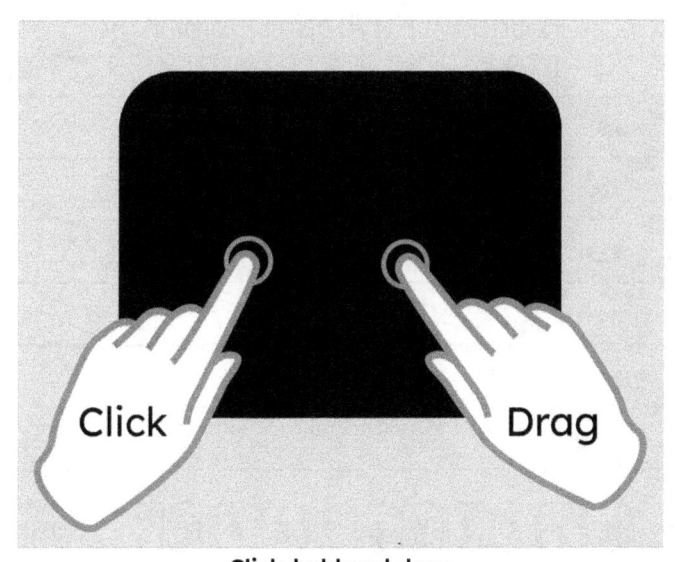

> **Jon**
>
> Wordwall.net is invaluable for helping students learn to use trackpads. This last year, I walked into a TK classroom, and the teacher warned me that the kids were "not very good on the trackpad." I had them open a Wordwall.net activity, using a QR code, and I said, "Let's see how good they are after five minutes," and they did a wonderful job. She was surprised and impressed. At no time was I required to give students a big lecture about trackpads. They figured them out very intuitively because they were interested in getting the result they wanted from the software.

Click-hold and drag

The second skill we like to teach students with the trackpad is the drag and drop skill. In the beginning, we find it is easier for students to use two hands to complete this process. With one hand, they push down and click, and with the other hand they drag the image or item around. Later on, students are able to move to one hand, but by starting with this two-hand method, we find they pick it up much faster.

We demonstrate this skill by putting our computer under the document camera. We also like to have students hold their hands up in the air and say, "Click and drag." We then like to open up a Seesaw activity, which uses the drag and drop skill. Have a few students practice it with the whole group. Then we send the students back to their seats to practice in small groups.

Typing

Typing can be a challenge. Look at a keyboard. To a young student, there is no rhyme or reason to how the keys are laid out. This is even more challenging to students who are just learning the names and shapes of letters. That said, the keyboard is another tool for teaching students the alphabet.

Rainbow Keyboard Color Key

Color	Letters or numbers	Keys
purple	q 1 2 9 0 p	search, tab, ;, enter
blue	a s w e 3 4 5 6 7 8 o l	', /, shift, :
green	z d r t y u i j k	,
yellow	x f g h m	ctrl, ctrl
orange	v b n c	alt, alt
red		

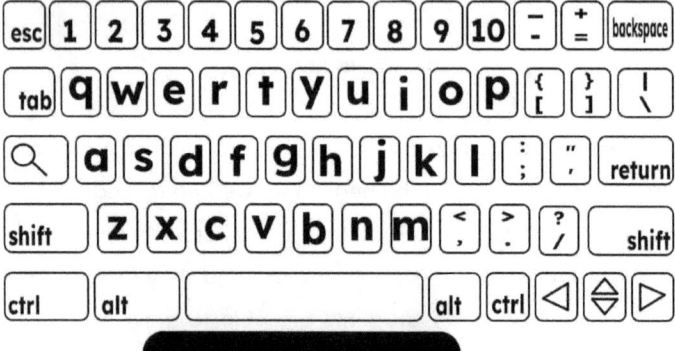

Rainbow keyboard

Want these resources? Visit primaryeduprotocols.us/resources.

Ben & Jenn

Beyond these fun activities, a little bit of old-fashioned keyboarding practice can go a long way to developing fluency. There are tons of great online programs with which students can practice.

Chapter 5 | Technology | 45

We have a few suggestions for jumpstarting students into typing. The first way is an activity called Rainbow Keyboard. For this activity, students are given a blank keyboard printout and a Rainbow Keyboard coloring key. Students color each key a different color, and in the end, the keyboard looks like a rainbow. This not only helps them learn the keys, it also helps with letter recognition.

This activity can then be taken to the next level with Rainbow Keyboard Sound Spelling. For this activity, students have to match the sound spelling card images with the keys of their keyboard. Talk about some good practice in phonics.

Rainbow Keyboard Sound Spelling

red						
orange						
yellow						
green						
blue						
purple						

Rainbow Keyboard Sound Spelling

Beyond the Rainbow Keyboard, we also love the ABC Challenge. For this activity, students use the note function in Seesaw; however, this can be any program that students can type in. Students have about five minutes to see how many times they can type their ABCs. When doing this, it is important to talk around the room and help students when they get stuck on a certain letter. After about a week of the ABC Challenge, students' keyboard fluency will improve.

Jon

The sooner a teacher teaches keyboarding, the sooner kids can type sentences and URLs! The correct letters and numbers, in the correct order, with punctuation is four standards. And the immediate feedback from typing programs speeds this process!

Ben & Jenn

Another fun way to practice keyboard skills is with one of our very own EduProtocols: Fast and Curious (chapter 10)! For this variation, use an online tool that has the option to type a response. Then, simply have a letter pop up as the question. Students will see the letter, and then they need to find it on their keyboard. Then, they complete the activity by typing the letter when they find it. For first and second grade, you can even do this for typing sight words. This way students get keyboarding practice while also practicing sight words, proper punctuation, capitalization, etc.

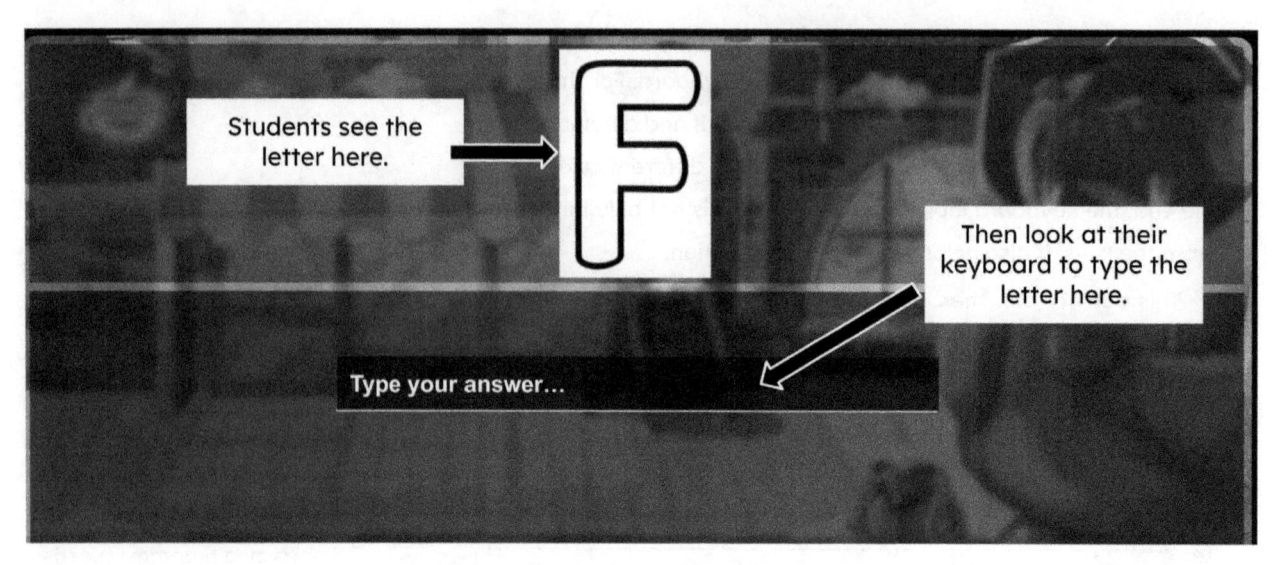

Use Fast and Curious to learn the keyboard.

The last suggestion we have is a Seesaw activity called Letter Hunt: Keyboard Edition (tinyurl.com/BenLetterHunt) that was designed by Ben. For this activity, students have to drag letters to where they belong on the keyboard. They can either look at their own keyboard on their device, or they can rely on a help section, from which they can drag out a completed keyboard. Students can then record themselves reviewing the letters on the keyboard.

Whatever method you choose for teaching keyboard skills, we suggest planning some extra time as students learn how to type. Once students learn the keys, their typing will improve. Of course, let us remind you that this is also a great way for students to learn the letters of the alphabet.

Jenn

You could also do this with students' names. Have a picture of a student with their name card for the question, and ask students to type that student's name for the answer. Now students are practicing keyboarding while also learning each other's names.

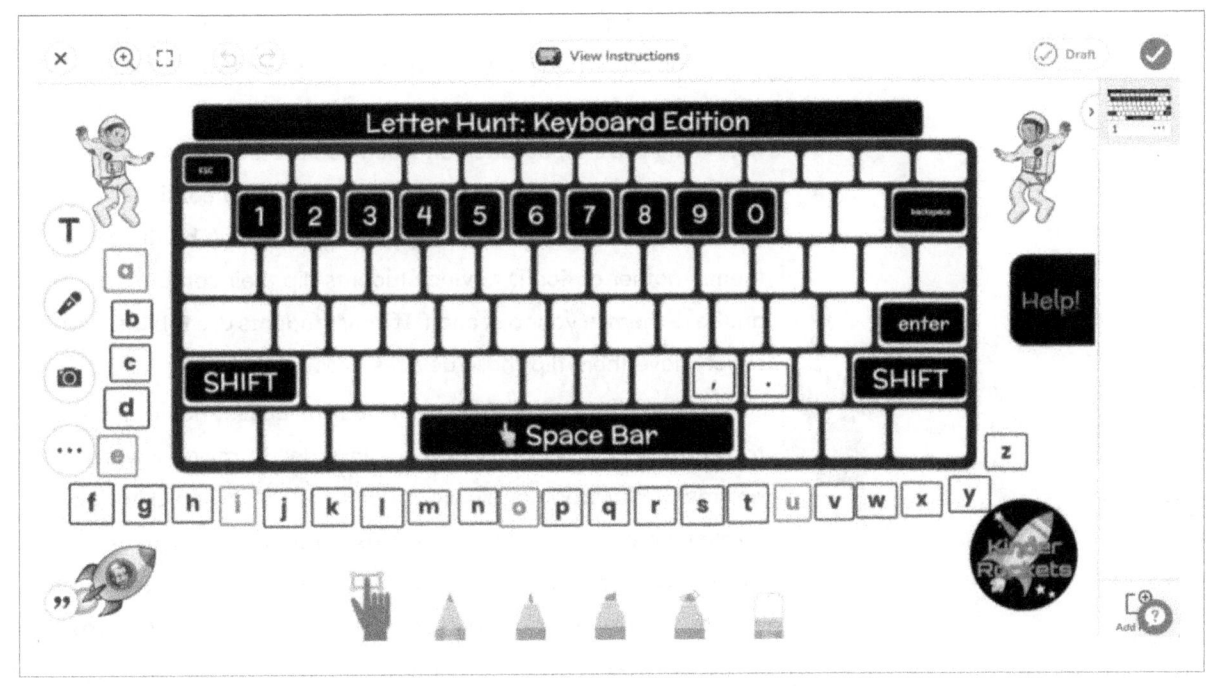

Letter Hunt: Keyboard Edition: As students learn the keyboard, they also learn the letters of the alphabet and the number line.

Building Routines for Technology Success

As students learn how to log in, use, and take care of their devices, it is important to build instructional routines around technology.

It can be hard enough to get students' attention when they are not using their computers, but it can even be more challenging when they are engaged with devices. Having a classroom signal can be super helpful in getting students to stop what they are doing and focus on you as their teacher. For example, if you have a call and response, or a sound like a chime, this is a great start. That said, sometimes it can be helpful for students to put their hands on their heads as part of the student response. This keeps their hands off their keyboard or devices. A fun call and response for this is to say, "Hands on top" with students responding, "Everybody stop."

> **Jenn**
> We have touch-screen tablets, so we tell students to make the screens black when we are not using them. They know this means they basically lock the screen rather than power it off, so the screen is black.

You can also refocus students using devices by directing them to "shark fin" their device by angling their screen to 45 degrees. We prefer this to having students close their device because it will mean they don't have to log back on when you are done talking; they can just tilt their device back up the 90 degrees and continue working. Also, when their screens are angled, students can't be distracted by them. Another option is having students flip their computers around and face them in your direction. If your students use tablets, you can simply have them flip those devices over.

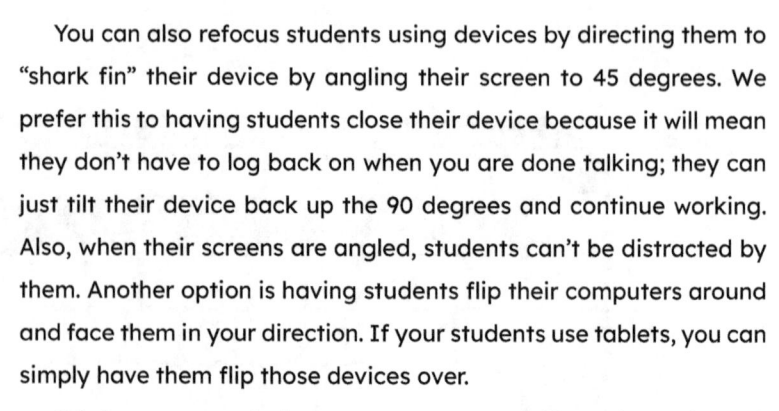

It is important to design a room you can quickly navigate through to see all of the students' screens in order to make sure they are on track. With traditional rows, it can be hard to quickly navigate through your students. Having tables or putting desks in groups can free up space and give you better access to all your students. Orienting your room well also allows you to quickly identify who needs help in the classroom.

Technology Helpers

Once you start using technology, you'll notice that some students are more ready to engage with devices than others.

One thing we know about technology is that it doesn't work 100 percent of the time. With only one teacher in the classroom, trying to fix all of the issues that may pop up with technology can be overwhelming. That is why we suggest identifying the students who are good with technology early on and enlisting those students as your technology helpers.

You can either have one technology helper per table group or two or three in the whole classroom. We like to have assigned helpers because this prevents the chaos that can ensue when everyone is trying to help everyone in the classroom. It can be helpful to show these students how to solve the most common issues you encounter, but you may find that they will discover how to solve problems on their own.

Jenn

Having students in groups is also helpful when you are engaging in Partner Talk. It gives them access to at least two sets of partners instead of just the person next to them.

Jenn

I strongly recommend having one technology helper per group. You may not always need that many, but it is nice to have to help prevent issues.

Jon

Let the kids help each other. There's no need to stop the whole class for peer-to-peer support!

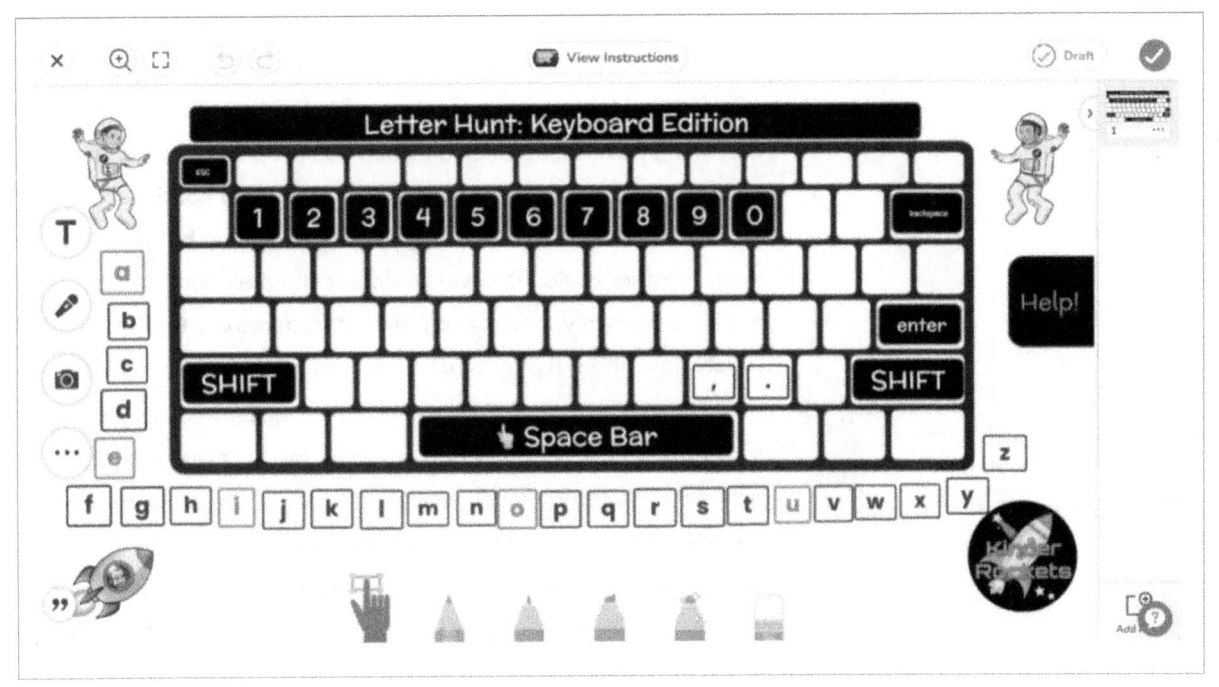

Letter Hunt: Keyboard Edition: As students learn the keyboard, they also learn the letters of the alphabet and the number line.

Building Routines for Technology Success

As students learn how to log in, use, and take care of their devices, it is important to build instructional routines around technology.

It can be hard enough to get students' attention when they are not using their computers, but it can even be more challenging when they are engaged with devices. Having a classroom signal can be super helpful in getting students to stop what they are doing and focus on you as their teacher. For example, if you have a call and response, or a sound like a chime, this is a great start. That said, sometimes it can be helpful for students to put their hands on their heads as part of the student response. This keeps their hands off their keyboard or devices. A fun call and response for this is to say, "Hands on top" with students responding, "Everybody stop."

> **Jenn**
> We have touch-screen tablets, so we tell students to make the screens black when we are not using them. They know this means they basically lock the screen rather than power it off, so the screen is black.

You can also refocus students using devices by directing them to "shark fin" their device by angling their screen to 45 degrees. We prefer this to having students close their device because it will mean they don't have to log back on when you are done talking; they can just tilt their device back up the 90 degrees and continue working. Also, when their screens are angled, students can't be distracted by them. Another option is having students flip their computers around and face them in your direction. If your students use tablets, you can simply have them flip those devices over.

It is important to design a room you can quickly navigate through to see all of the students' screens in order to make sure they are on track. With traditional rows, it can be hard to quickly navigate through your students. Having tables or putting desks in groups can free up space and give you better access to all your students. Orienting your room well also allows you to quickly identify who needs help in the classroom.

Technology Helpers

Once you start using technology, you'll notice that some students are more ready to engage with devices than others.

One thing we know about technology is that it doesn't work 100 percent of the time. With only one teacher in the classroom, trying to fix all of the issues that may pop up with technology can be overwhelming. That is why we suggest identifying the students who are good with technology early on and enlisting those students as your technology helpers.

You can either have one technology helper per table group or two or three in the whole classroom. We like to have assigned helpers because this prevents the chaos that can ensue when everyone is trying to help everyone in the classroom. It can be helpful to show these students how to solve the most common issues you encounter, but you may find that they will discover how to solve problems on their own.

> **Jenn**
>
> Having students in groups is also helpful when you are engaging in Partner Talk. It gives them access to at least two sets of partners instead of just the person next to them.

> **Jenn**
>
> I strongly recommend having one technology helper per group. You may not always need that many, but it is nice to have to help prevent issues.

> **Jon**
>
> Let the kids help each other. There's no need to stop the whole class for peer-to-peer support!

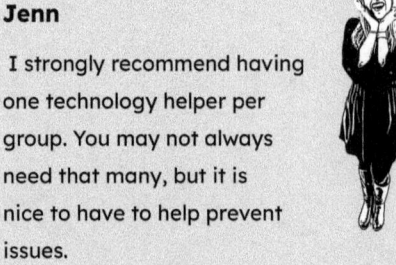

Chapter 6
Starting with Seesaw

In chapter 3 we explained why we love Seesaw so much and think it is an amazing tool all around, especially for introducing technology skills and EduProtocols. Now, let's dive into how to get started with the app as part of Smart Start.

What is one thing you always wish you had more of in the classroom? We can almost guarantee the answer is time. It always seems like time goes fast and we need more of it. As a result, we believe the best way to start with Seesaw is to use it to teach skills in context. What exactly does this mean?

Teaching skills in context means teaching students how to use Seesaw tools within the context of classroom work, rather than in isolation. For example, you might want to introduce students to using the photo tool by having them take a selfie. There is nothing wrong with this. It is actually a fun activity, and it does help students learn how to use the tool.

However, a better introduction to Seesaw's photo function would be to teach it in context. For example, when teaching students how to use the photo tools to take a selfie, focus on using selfies as a way for students to get to know each other; this will help to build a classroom community. Additionally, focus on key skills, like taking a good picture. Model what a good picture looks like so that students will learn how to fill the frame, make sure the whole item is in the picture, and focus the image.

Another option would be to have students use the photo tool to take a picture of something they made. Have students use Lego or

> **Ben & Jenn**
> Don't use Seesaw? No worries! A lot of what we talk about here can be transferred to other applications or programs.

> **Jenn**
> In fact, it is a building block for when we do Sketch and Tell, Emoji Writing, MathReps, and so many more!

> **Jenn**
> Pro tip. When using a Chromebook or laptop, teach students how to tap the spacebar to take a picture. This can be much easier than trying to use the touchpad.

Play-Doh to build something or construct their name. Then teach them how to use the photo tool to take a picture of it.

Ben & Jenn

Want to learn more about Build and Tell? Check out chapter 12.

Jenn

This introductory activity is awesome because it is automatically differentiated. Students can type up to the numbers they know. If they can type all the way to 120, then great! If not, that's okay too.

Ben

Ask students to do some of these same activities on the last day of school. It is amazing to show students how much they have grown.

Activity Ideas for Introducing Seesaw Tools	
Photo	• Have students take a first day of school picture. • Take a picture of students making a happy choice and a sad choice in school. • Have students find an item that starts with a given letter. • Have students do a Directed Drawing and take a picture of it.
Video	• Have students make a video of a procedure or a routine. • Have students make a video introducing a classmate. • Ask students to complete an "about me" activity on paper, and then have students record themselves sharing about the activity. • Let students build a number with Unifix cubes, and record a video showing what number they made and count the cubes.
Drawing	• Have students draw a picture of themselves on the first day of school. • Invite students to draw a picture of what they want to be when they grow up. • Read a story and then have students draw the character of the story. • Use the Would You Rather slides and then have students draw a picture about which item they would rather have.
Note	• Have students type their first name. • Ask students to type the ABCs. • Instruct students to type sight words. • Introduce the number line on the keyboard and have students type numbers.

Layer Skills

Another important way to start with Seesaw is to layer skills. In the example, students can use the camera in Seesaw to take a selfie. To layer skills, students can then use labels to type their name or adjectives to describe themselves. Then, they can use drawing tools to draw a costume over themselves or use the microphone to tell important details.

If you direct students to build something and take a photo of it, then layer skills by having students use labels to explain what they made, use the microphone to tell about what they made, or use the pens to draw an addition to what they made. For example, if they made their name with Play-Doh, students could take a picture and then use pens to write their name or challenge themselves to write their last name.

The great thing about Seesaw is there are so many ways you can introduce the app's tools and layer them as you go. If students aren't familiar with a tool, layering skills or tools one at a time can really help students master the tool more quickly. Continue layering and modeling, layering and modeling, until you have introduced all of Seesaw's tools. Just as you have to do rep after rep for EduProtocols, you should do the same with Seesaw. Repeat, model, repeat, until students are mastering their technology skills with Seesaw. Then, when they have it down, life will be much easier.

Do you want even more ideas on how to get started with Seesaw? Check out our secret webpage that breaks down Seesaw even more!

Ben

I almost always use the creative canvas and then have students add the video or photo inside of the canvas. That doesn't mean I don't ever use the video or photo, but often the activities my students complete include adding a video or photo, so I try to get them used to that ASAP.

Ben

One of my favorite introductory activities is having students take a selfie and then draw on top of the picture to turn themselves into astronauts. This reinforces the context of our classroom because we are Kinder Rockets. Plus, students are layering the skills they have learned.

Jenn

When it comes to introducing multiple pages, you can do that right away in second grade, but in first grade, it would be good to wait until you lay some foundations for the other tools within Seesaw.

Ben

The first activities I do are typically one-page activities. After students get used to the one-page activity, I slowly add a few pages at a time. Adding too many pages at the beginning can be overwhelming for some students, so it's best to keep it short and sweet.

Extended Content:
Smart Start: Starting with Seesaw

Starting with Seesaw with scaffolded instruction from the beginning of the year can help students be successful all year long. Even if you don't use Seesaw, there are some tips and ideas that can be implemented in other platforms.

In the extended content, you'll get:
- ★ Modeling Seesaw activities
- ★ Using Seesaw for Directed Drawing
- ★ Teaching students new skills
- ★ Teaching students how to comment and interact with each other

tinyurl.com/StartingWithSeesaw
Password: 73468

Chapter 7
Classroom Introduction to Smart Start

In the TK–2 classroom, Smart Start is extra important because it is often the students' first experience with school. Young learners are learning not only academic standards but also major skills such as collaboration, cooperation, following routines, and so much more. Additionally, younger students need to feel safe and have an environment that makes learning possible and also engaging and fun. Smart Start helps you do just that.

Essentially, Smart Start looks different in the TK–2 classroom because students are learning how to be students. Instead of having a set schedule for the first week or two of school, where a ton of different EduProtocols are used, many Smart Start activities will lead up to EduProtocols. For example, we first run Directed Drawing to build the skills for the Sketch and Tell EduProtocol. However, in other cases, you can jump right into a given EduProtocol. For example, you can introduce Fast and Curious as early as day one as a way for students to get to know you, their teacher.

Below you'll find suggested sequences of Smart Start activities and EduProtocols that are appropriate for each TK–2 grade level. The activities and EduProtocols themselves will follow.

As you'll see, we reference a few EduProtocols that are not covered in this book. You can always reference previous field guides to get more information on these. The Frayer model is available in *The EduProtocol Field Guide, Book One*. Thin Slides, meanwhile, is found in *The EduProtocol Field Guide, Book Two*.

Kindergarten Smart Start
tinyurl.com/kindersmartstart

Kindergarten Smart Start
Week at a Glance

The first few days of kindergarten can be a little bit like herding cats. This EduProtocol Smart Start can make it a little bit easier. Keep in mind that you don't need to do *all* of the EduProtocols each day, but they are options that you can mix and match. We know you will have plenty of other routines and expectations to review as well. Also make sure to visit the different Smart Starts via the QR code or URLs because we link many resources in these documents.

Day 1	• Fast and Curious: Get to Know the Teacher (Whole Group) • Mini MathReps: My Number Booklet #1 • Sketch and Tell: Directed Drawing—My First Day of Kindergarten • Sketch and Tell: Directed Drawing—Rocket on Paper • Would You Rather: Draw on a Sticky Note, Partner Share, Graph Results • Design Think Challenge: Play-Doh Routines
Day 2	• Fast and Curious: Get to Know the Teacher (Whole Group) • Mini MathReps: My Number Booklet #2 • Sketch and Tell: Directed Drawing—Rocket on Seesaw • Would You Rather: Draw on a Sticky Note, Partner Share, Graph Results • Design Think Challenge: Play-Doh Snakes & Spheres

| Day 3 | • Fast and Curious: Get to Know the Teacher (Whole Group)
• Mini MathReps: My Number Booklet #3
• Sketch and Tell: Directed Drawing—Rainbow on Paper
• Would You Rather: Draw on a Sticky Note, Partner Share, Graph Results
• Design Think Challenge: Play-Doh Make a Rocket |
|---|---|
| Day 4 | • Fast and Curious: Get to Know Your Classmates (Whole Group)
• Mini MathReps: My Number Booklet #4
• Sketch and Tell: Directed Drawing—Rainbow on Seesaw
• Would You Rather: Draw on a Sticky Note, Partner Share, Graph Results
• Little p*ARTS: Nouns and Verbs (Whole Group)
• Design Think Challenge: Play-Doh Make an Astronaut |
| Day 5 | • Fast and Curious: Get to Know Your Classmates (Whole Group)
• Mini MathReps: My Number Booklet #5
• Sketch and Tell: Directed Drawing—Rainbow with Watercolors
• Would You Rather: Draw on a Sticky Note, Partner Share, Graph Results
• Little p*ARTS: Nouns and Verbs
• Design Think Challenge: Play-Doh You Choose |

First-Grade Smart Start Week at a Glance

The first-grade week at a glance is very similar to the kindergarten version. However, this one is a little less teacher led, and there are a

First-Grade Smart Start

tinyurl.com/1smartstart

few different activities. However, the general idea is very similar. See a progression?

Day 1	• Fast and Curious: Get to Know the Teacher • MathReps # of the Day (1) • Random Emoji: Would You Rather • Sketch and Tell: Directed Draw & Tell about It • Design Thinking Challenge: Play-Doh
Day 2	• Fast and Curious: Get to Know the Teacher • MathReps # of the Day (2) • Random Emoji: Would You Rather • Sketch and Tell: Directed Draw & Tell about It • Design Thinking Challenge: Play-Doh
Day 3	• Fast and Curious: Get to Know Your Classmates • MathReps # of the Day (3) • Random Emoji: Would You Rather • Sketch and Tell: Directed Draw & Tell about It • Design Thinking Challenge: Lego
Day 4	• Fast and Curious: Get to Know Your Classmates • MathReps # of the Day (4) • Random Emoji: Would You Rather • Sketch and Tell: Directed Draw & Tell about It • Design Thinking Challenge: Lego
Day 5	• Fast and Curious: Get to Know Your Classmates • MathReps # of the Day (5) • Random Emoji: Would You Rather • Sketch and Tell: Directed Draw & Tell about It • Design Thinking Challenge: Student Choice

Second-Grade Smart Start

tinyurl.com/2smartstart

Second-Grade Smart Start Week at a Glance

The second-grade week at a glance is very similar to the first-grade week at a glance. However, it takes it to the next level by integrating first-grade spiral review MathReps. Another change is with the Sketch and Tell aspect. Instead of doing a directed draw each day, they dive into the Sketch and Tell protocol sooner by sketching to tell about themselves.

Day 1	• Fast and Curious: Get to Know the Teacher • MathReps First-Grade Spiral Review • Random Emoji: Would You Rather • Sketch and Tell: Directed Draw & Tell about It • Design Thinking Challenge: Play-Doh
Day 2	• Fast and Curious: Get to Know the Teacher • MathReps First-Grade Spiral Review • Random Emoji: Would You Rather • Sketch and Tell: Directed Draw & Tell about It • Design Thinking Challenge: Play-Doh
Day 3	• Fast and Curious: Get to Know Your Classmates • MathReps First-Grade Spiral Review • Random Emoji: Would You Rather • Sketch and Tell: Something That Makes You Happy • Design Thinking Challenge: Lego
Day 4	• Fast and Curious: Get to Know Your Classmates • MathReps First-Grade Spiral Review • Random Emoji: Would You Rather • Sketch and Tell: An Activity You Enjoy • Design Thinking Challenge: Lego
Day 5	• Fast and Curious: Get to Know Your Classmates • MathReps First-Grade Spiral Review • Random Emoji: Would You Rather • Sketch and Tell: Your Family • Design Thinking Challenge: Student Choice

Now that you have an idea how our first week is structured, let's go ahead and get a better idea of what these EduProtocols look

TK–2 Smart Start Resources

tinyurl.com/K2SmartStart

like. After we do a deep dive into each EduProtocol, we will circle back to the how to Smart Start with the various EduProtocols themselves.

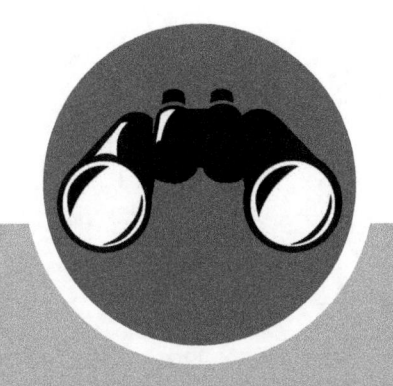

SECTION 3

EduProtocols

Chapter 8
Little p*ARTS EduProtocol

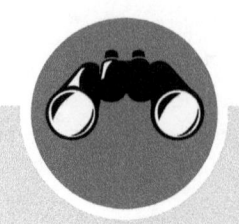

Anyone who steps into a primary classroom knows that young learners are not ready to master the full eight parts of speech, yet they are expected to learn and use them in both speaking and writing, according to the Common Core language standards. Parts of speech also make students' speaking and writing more interesting. Think about it. Which sentence is more interesting?

- The crab crawls.
- The bright red crab crawls quickly on the sand.

Learning the parts of speech in context helps students become more efficient and creative writers by adding more or various parts of speech into their writing and speaking.

A modified version of the 8 p*ARTS of Speech EduProtocol, called Little p*ARTS, can help younger students learn language, make writing more interesting, and master important language and writing standards. Little p*ARTS to the rescue!

Academic Goals

- Students master the parts of speech
- Students understand how the parts of speech work together
- Students develop oral and written language
- Students use the parts of speech to write simple and expanded sentences leading up to a paragraph

Jon

Ben's approach to Little p*ARTS is extremely important. You see, when kids only do sentence frames in early grades, when they get to fourth, fifth, or sixth grade, they aren't used to capitalizing, using an ending punctuation, or creating a sentence. Ben's Little p*ARTS approach means students are responsible for the entire sentence, but in a fun, scaffolded way.

Teacher Big Ideas

- Parts of speech work together, not separately.
- Students master their language and grammar skills.
- Students use the parts of speech to write.
- Students start small, with 2-3 parts, then add in more as they go. You can count punctuation as a part of speech.

Original EduProtocol: The 8 p*ARTS of Speech

Traditionally, this EduProtocol centers around getting students to practice the eight parts of speech all at once. To get started, show the class a highly engaging picture. Together, unpack the different parts of speech evident in the picture, putting them together to form a complete paragraph with interesting sentences.

1. Instead of doing one skill at a time, with 8 p*ARTs, we are going to teach kids a bundle of skills at once (ideally all 8), with a creativity element.
2. First, find a fun, grade-level appropriate image or GIF.
3. On day one, supply the students with the answers (I do), making sure they copy along. Keep the paper (copied to both sides) for tomorrow's use.
4. On day two, use a new fun picture or GIF, and give the students one example in each part of speech, gathering other examples from the students collaboratively (we do).
5. Repeat this process daily, slowly removing the supports. For best results, you'll want to do 8 p*ARTS/Little p*ARTS at least three times a week for 3-4 weeks.
6. Daily grades: If students complete the entire page, they get five points, even if a couple are incorrect. Note the patterns where kids are struggling and do a micro-lesson or Fast and Curious before the next round.
7. Weekly grades: Once a week, we do an 8 p*ARTS by ourselves for a classic numeric grade.

8. The 8 p*ARTS cycle completes with a final assessment. Kids will find their own picture and do the entire process on their own.

Three	Word	Sentence
Frogs	act	silly.

Verbs	Adverbs

Write a Paragraph using at least ONE of each part of speech. Highlight using the color coding.

Nouns (one proper)	Adjectives

Prepositions

Under, on top of, beneath

Interjections

Conjunctions

Pronouns

Create a Simile

The original 8 p*ARTS of Speech template

Ben's Way (Kindergarten)

I like to start writing sentences in kindergarten as soon as possible. I love Little p*ARTS, as a variation of 8 p*ARTS of Speech, because it gives some great scaffolding that will help young learners put together some basic sentences with lots of room for growth. This year, I decided to try something new with Little p*ARTS and incorporate Jenn's awesome idea: I decided to break the protocol down even more, and just start with nouns and verbs.

Chapter 8 | Little p*ARTS EduProtocol | 63

Noun and Verbs: A modified 8 p*ARTS of Speech for kindergarten

I took a step back from sentences to just nouns and verbs because not enough of my students understood what a complete sentence was. Breaking it into smaller learning chunks provided the scaffolding I needed to ensure the success of more students. As a bonus, by focusing on individual words, we are able to hit phonics as hard as we are writing, and we can ramp up the protocol even quicker. As a super bonus, we still do quite a bit of writing for the beginning of the year, and we can use our writing to create sentences orally.

When we begin Little p*ARTS, I usually start with a shared writing experience, in which I, the teacher, hold the pen, while the students help contribute different ideas. Sometimes I will recreate the EduProtocol template on chart paper, and sometimes I will put the template under a document camera.

Similar to the original 8 p*ARTS EduProtocol, I start with a picture or animated GIF; however, I don't always start with super funny, engaging pictures. Instead, I typically start with animal pictures because many students love animals and have some background vocabulary to pull from. Also, in the beginning we tend to stick to one noun, like *bear*, and just change up the verbs. This helps keep the lesson crisp and students engaged, as phonics skills are woven into the

Jenn

I have found that first graders are really intimidated by the writing process. That is why when I first start with Little p*ARTS, I start with just a few parts of speech to get them used to it and take some fear away. However, after one or two weeks of doing the EduProtocol without the writing component, we quickly move on to sentence writing.

Ben

After a few reps with two parts of speech, I move right into using three parts of speech by adding punctuation. With this addition, I also make sure to include some lines on the bottom for writing a sentence.

lesson as we write. I try to keep these lessons to five or ten minutes to maximize student attention since they are only watching and not actively writing.

> **Ben**
> Sometimes when the picture is too funny, my students can't stop laughing. This is especially true in the beginning of the year, when five-year-old students are still learning how to be students. However, if you are looking for some interesting pictures, you can visit: eduprotocols.com/8parts.

Three-part sentence modification with the ending punctuation

After a few reps with just me holding the pen, students can then bring a clipboard to the carpet and will get their own graphic organizer. They can then start to write on their own paper, and we complete the template as a group; everyone writes together. Once students have a decent understanding of nouns and verbs, I make a quick transition into a three-part sentence made up of nouns, verbs, and punctuation. I also add a section on the paper so that students can write one or two sentences to really put it all together.

As the year progresses and students are beginning to write words, we move this template from a shared writing experience to an interactive writing experience. With the interactive writing experience, the students do more of the writing on the template as we are working together to identify nouns and verbs. I will also start to show different images or GIFs other than animals. I also love to show students book covers before we read the book. This allows us to make predictions about what we are going to read as well as build vocabulary.

🖐 4 Part Sentence			Name: _____
Adjective 👁👁🤚✋	Noun 👥📍🚀	Verb 🏃👥🐎	. ? !

A four-part sentence modification with ending punctuation

When students begin to master this EduProtocol and start to write on their own, this is a great activity to transition into centers. You can show students a picture and have them go to town. You can also have students pull words from a vocabulary wall to create their own silly sentences. Further, you can keep adding other parts of speech for when you think your students are ready. Keep pushing them ahead and make sure they are creating interesting sentences.

Preparation

1. Choose your Little p*ARTS template. You can use one of my paper versions, make your own version to fit your class, or adapt Jenn's Seesaw versions to fit your needs.
2. Find a picture, GIF, or video you want to use—really any multimedia will do. As I mentioned above, book covers, or even pages from picture books can be a great way to start. I also like to find live streams of animals, like those at the Monterey Bay Aquarium, because they are super interesting to students. The moral of the story is to find something that will interest and engage your students.

Ben

Using book covers is one of my favorite ways to use this protocol. We hit multiple standards at once. Students get to make predictions about the text we are reading. Additionally, they start building vocabulary about the text. Plus, I can slip this protocol into something I am already doing.

Jenn

I also love using images directly from books and/or their covers. I specifically love taking books from our curriculum, so instead of making this "one more thing," it is part of a natural classroom flow.

Marlena

Using book covers and book images is a wonderful first step toward using 8 p*ARTS in the content areas! Next up, science and social studies!

3. Make copies of your template. I like to make 100–200 copies of a template at a time since I know I will be using it for a few reps.

Instructions

1. Display your multimedia for the day. This can be an image, video, or GIF. Have students evaluate what they see. Students can share with a partner or with the whole class. You can ask, "What do you notice, and what do you wonder?"
2. Get students' brains ready for Little p*ARTS! Remind students about the parts of speech they will focus on, then give a quick definition of each part of speech. Sometimes, I use a Google Slides deck with some quick examples. Review the parts of speech on the template you are using, referencing what you just reviewed.

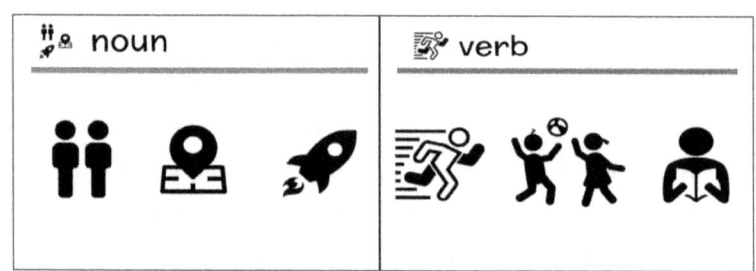

A slide deck reviewing the parts of speech for a simple 8 p*ARTS of Speech round

3. Have students identify the part of speech you are focusing on. You can do it as a class, as partners, or a mixture of the two. As students identify the parts of speech in context, you can work in your phonics practice as time allows. It helps to do some oral practice first before you actually put pen to paper.
4. Start writing down the parts of speech! There are a few options when you are writing on the teacher template. You can write as a shared writing model (you hold the pen), or students can write in an interactive writing model (student holds the pen).

Ben

Depending on your flow, steps 1 and 2 can be switched. Sometimes, I like to use the image to build some intrigue, while other times I review the Little p*ARTS, and that way I can jump right into the image.

Ben

Just like I can flip step 1 and step 2, you can decide if you want to start by identifying the noun or the verb. Sometimes I like to start with the verb because it is easier to identify the noun when it is paired with the action. For example, "What action do you see? Who or what is doing the action?" Some nouns that kids identify don't have too many easily identifiable actions. For example, the action of a rock, a bed, or a chair is not obvious.

5. As the year progresses, I like to have all students try writing on their templates first, before they see each word written on the teacher template. Then, only after students write on their template, we write the word on the teacher template. I also work in partner sharing as time allows so students can check the words they are writing.

6. Read and review! Once you have written down the words for the parts of speech, it's time to read over what your class wrote. We try to focus on reading and identifying sounds rather than relying on rote memorization. You can ask questions like, "What word is this?" and "How do you know?" It is also helpful to keep referencing the media you used for the words and match the words they wrote as you are reading them.

7. Write your sentences. Now that you have reviewed the words your class wrote, it is time to pick your sentences. You can either write directly across if you are using my template or choose nouns and verbs from different rows. You can write a sentence that makes sense or a silly sentence, mixing and matching different parts of speech. The most important part for me is that students know what they are writing. As mentioned above, how you write the sentences, as far as who is doing the work, will depend on the time of year. We progress from copying, to writing together, to students writing independently. I also try to encourage students to make sure to go back and reread what they wrote.

8. Take time to share. If you are short on time, you can have students turn in their work. If not, you have a few options as far as sharing what students wrote. Of course, thinking about a blended model, students can record in Seesaw with a picture and microphone or a video. Additionally, students could share with partners or in small groups. Finally, students can come up and read what they wrote under the document camera.

Ben

Color coding your parts of speech can help them stick even more. Some programs already have their own colors, or you can use your own as long as you stay consistent.

Jenn

I LOVE color coding! Students learn the colors, and it really solidifies the parts of speech for them. Example: verbs are green because green means go, and verbs are actions.

Marlena

When sharing, I like to have students who finish come up and read their sentence or paragraph to the class while other students needing more time are finishing up. We do this from the front of the room while everyone is still at their desks. I find that this keeps the early finishers engaged while eking out a little more writing time for those who need it.

Jenn's Way (1st-2nd)

When I do this EduProtocol, I start with two parts of speech. I usually start with nouns and verbs because those are the two main parts of speech we really focus on in the beginning of our year. As the year goes on, we are able to add to these initial parts of speech.

For example, once we mostly master nouns and verbs, we add in adjectives to give us three parts of speech. Then at some point we start talking about common and proper nouns. When this starts, I change the activity to four parts of speech: proper nouns, common nouns, adjectives, and verbs. Then we usually introduce pronouns, which gives us five parts of speech. Each time we introduce a new part of speech, I either add it to our template, or I change one out.

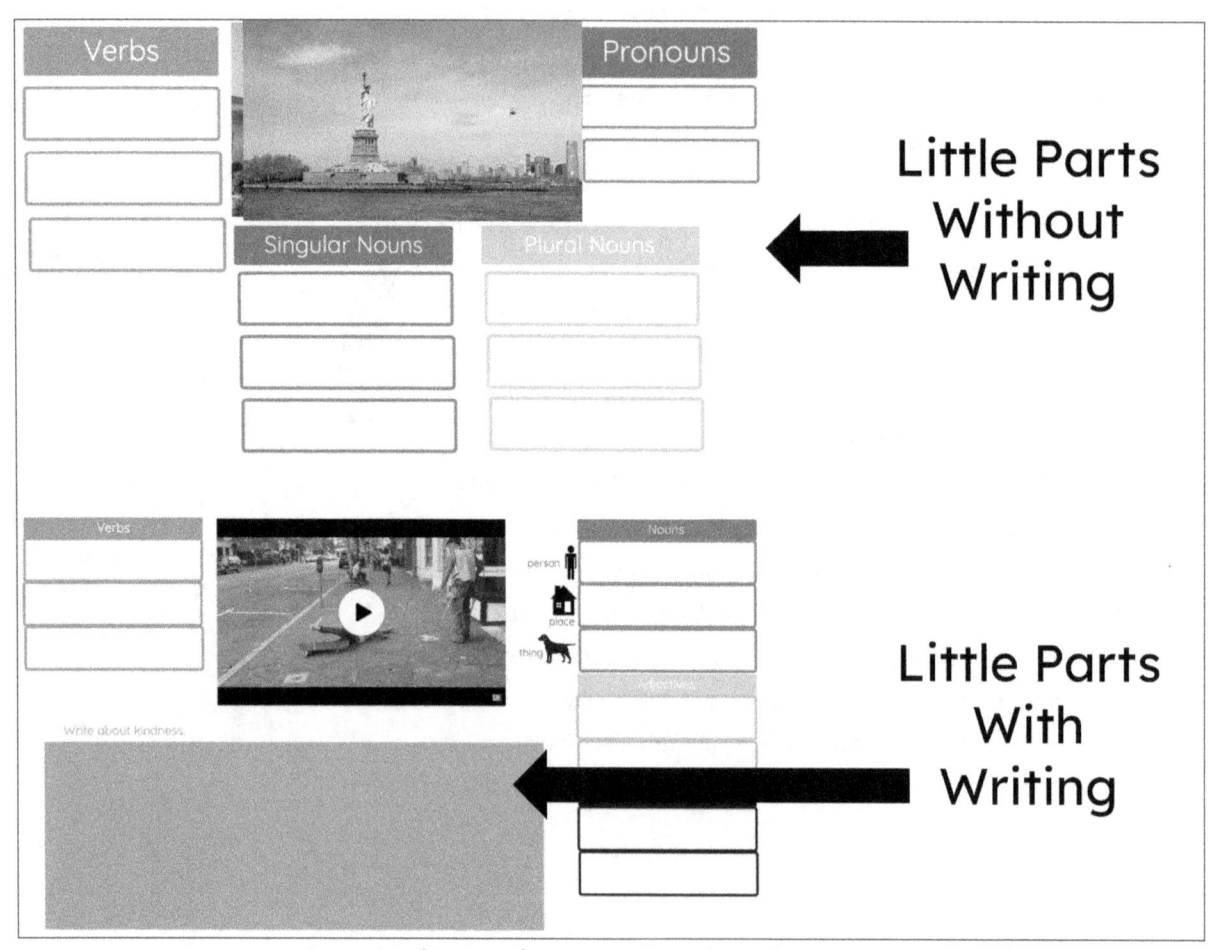

A progression from just parts of speech to include sentence writing

As you can see, I start with nouns, but when I add common and proper nouns, I get rid of the "regular" noun.

Another key point of this EduProtocol is the focus on writing. The purpose of Little p*ARTS is not just to learn the parts of speech but also to learn how they work together to form writing.

With the original version of 8 p*ARTS of Speech, students complete eight parts of speech and then write a paragraph (or more) using the different parts of speech. However, in my classroom, I start with writing one sentence about the picture. Think about how we as teachers start with simple sentences and then work on expanding sentences using the parts of speech. Well, this protocol helps us to really teach that breakdown in a way that makes sense to students.

As students master the skill of sentence writing, we start writing two sentences, then three, and so on until we get our paragraph. Additionally, as we add more parts of speech, we expand our sentences. For example, in the first couple of weeks, we might write a sentence as simple as "The dog runs." However, as we add more parts of speech, we expand our sentences to "The brown dog runs in the yard." Students learn how to expand their sentences in a more organic way that makes sense to them. As they add more sentences, it might say, "The brown dog runs in the yard. He chases the small kid. He swims in the big pool." In first grade, we are writing our paragraphs before winter break because it makes sense and shows students how components of language work together!

We have found that it takes about 5-10 times together for the students to really understand what to do. However, it varies with each class and sometimes even from one student to the next. After doing this protocol together a few times, have the kids work with partners to complete the EduProtocol. Since students have already learned how to start the collaboration process and know the template, transitioning to doing this with partners is very smooth. This becomes a center that students complete three times a week.

As an assessment, Little p*ARTS of Speech can also periodically be assigned as an independent activity to use as an assessment. What better way to assess students than with a template they are

> **Ben**
>
> Jenn brings up a great point about students really internalizing the different parts of speech in context. Nearly every sentence contains nouns and verbs, and students start noticing these when they are reading and writing in other areas. This protocol helps cement the building blocks of writing.

> **Jenn**
>
> You don't have to limit the students. If they want to write more, why not let them? But don't be afraid to start small and work your way up. Little p*ARTS = automatic differentiation.

> **Jenn**
>
> I usually do this protocol together with students five to ten times before I have students work with a partner, then independently. Once students go to the independent stage, I work with the few who need more help in a small group. IMMEDIATE FEEDBACK.

> **Jon**
>
> In a Little p*ARTS activity, the kids are writing for each other. Their work doesn't go in a bin. We celebrate it, enjoy it, and relish it, immediately.

familiar with? Assessments like these show what the students know about the content.

Preparation

- Create the Little p*ARTS of Speech template in any program you want! Better yet, find a premade template. There are so many out there that are ready to go!

- Find an image or GIF you want to use. You can google it or take a screenshot from some of your mandatory curriculum books. I have found that some of the books we are required to use for ELA, Science, or Social Studies have some pretty awesome visuals. Add the image to the template.

- Assign the template to your students. You can use a digital template, or you can do this directly on paper. The steps are the same, just print the template and pass it out.

Instructions

1. On their computers, students open up the protocol with you.
2. Look at the picture together. Review one of the parts of speech. For example, review that nouns are people, places, and things. Ask students to look at the picture and find some nouns. Give students time to think. Have students share some nouns. Show them how to add those nouns to the template and have them do it with you!
3. Go to the next part of speech. For example, verbs. Review what a verb is. Have students look at the picture and share out verbs, the same way you did with nouns. Add these to the template together. Complete this process for all the parts of speech.
4. Direct students to use the parts of speech to write a simple sentence. For example, "The silly baby made a mess with the spaghetti."
5. As students master the concept, transition to a partner activity. This variation is great for a center activity!

Ben

Thinking time is super important for students. They need to do their own thinking because we won't always be there for them.

Ben & Jenn

The transition is smooth for most but there may be students who need more help. Those are the students we make sure we really focus on to help them master this. An easy way to do this is to quickly divide the work into two piles after students are done. One for students who need more support and one for students who are ready to rock.

Jenn

You can ask students to find nouns and share them with a partner. This is great to get them practicing working with a partner, as eventually they will be doing this with partners only.

Jenn

As students master this, slowly add more writing and other parts of speech until students are eventually writing one paragraph using all eight parts of speech.

6. As students master this EduProtocol in partners, it can also be used as an independent activity and/or assessment.

Find the Random Emoji Generator at eduprotocols.com/class.

Extended Content:
Little p*ARTS

Little p*ARTS is a great way to build grammar, sentence, and paragraph proficiency. Seesaw allows us to give students the multimedia to review as they need and use language in multiple ways.

In the extended content, you'll get:
- ★ How we use Seesaw to build even more language in the Little p*ARTS EduProtocol
- ★ How to edit and create templates for Little p*ARTS in Seesaw
- ★ Special tips and tricks to help meet the needs of all students with Seesaw tools
- ★ Templates, resources, student examples, and more

My notes:

How It Looks in Seesaw	Templates & Resources	Student Examples
tinyurl.com/lpSeesaw Password: 73468	tinyurl.com/LittlePartsFolder	tinyurl.com/LittlePartsExamples

Chapter 9
Little Random Emoji Writing EduProtocol

I am going to tell you about avocados. Firstly, avocados are delicious. Secondly, they grow on trees. Thirdly, you use them to make guacamole. This is my paragraph about avocados.

Sound familiar?

Most, if not all, of us have read numerous hamburger-style paragraphs with the same introduction sentence, a few supporting details, and the same closing sentence. Although this may be a great starting point, as our TK–2 students need modeling and structures to learn how to write, it is not a structure that really teaches writing. Do kids ask to write these? Do they really learn how to write authentically this way? No and no!

This type of writing does not engage students, it does not spark their creativity, and it does not teach them to truly write. What does teach them how to write and spark their creativity? The Random Emoji Power Paragraph!

Academic Goals

- Students focus writing on a specific topic and pursue an idea
- Students are empowered as critical and creative thinkers
- Students develop writing skills and build writing fluency
- Students build language, including mastering speaking and listening skills

Marlena
Unfortunately, once students learn formula writing in primary, some never move past it! I've seen sixth graders still writing firstly, secondly, thirdly, lastly.

Jon
I created the Random Emoji Power Paragraph because once we do the hamburger, there's not another higher-level model, so we just keep hamburgering!

Teacher Big Ideas

- Students must get used to "writing from a prompt," as they never know what emojis are going to show up.
- Students ask to write and go through the editing process in real time.
- Immediate feedback, less grading = more productive.
- Students produce different products, which allows for reflection and discussion.

Original EduProtocol: The Random Emoji Power Paragraph

The Random Emoji Power Paragraph started as a way to increase creativity when writing a paragraph in a fun and engaging way. Jon Corippo saw the simple elegance of random emoji generators and soon developed a free random emoji generator with school-appropriate emojis. The Random Emoji Power Paragraph, using random emojis, was inspired by the key concept from Robert Pinckert that writing a paragraph was pursuing an idea, not just following a specific format, and basically listing information.

In the original protocol, students will use Socrative (or another tool that allows them to quickly see and share each other's prompts) to write a paragraph as emojis are revealed. The idea is to reveal one emoji at a time and have students add to their writing as emojis are revealed. Revealing one emoji at a time helps the academic load feel light. This will help them pursue an idea in a paragraph rather than randomly writing sentences. At the end, students will read their paragraphs to the group and vote to determine their favorite. The best part? In a class of thirty students, you get thirty different paragraphs instead of the same one thirty times.

Steps

1. Go to www.socrative.com (or the tool of your choice) and launch a Short Answer question or any open-ended quiz

where you and the kids can see immediate results of their writing.

2. Invite students and get them in the quiz.
3. Open the EduProtocols Random Emoji Generator (eduprotocols.com/class) and project it on your screen.
4. Generate the first emoji and have students begin their writing, one sentence at a time.
5. Generate the next emoji and have students connect it to their first sentence. The key skill is pursuing an idea.
6. Continue for a total of 3–5 emojis and have students submit their writing.
7. Give students a few minutes to read and rate as many Random Emoji Power Paragraphs as they can, and to vote for examples they want the teacher to read.
8. Prep for tomorrow: Simply make a mental note of two or three of the most common errors to mini-teach before tomorrow's reps.
9. Idea for a final assessment: Let kids pick their own emoji!

Ben's Way (Kindergarten)

My first attempt at emoji writing happened during my time as a virtual teacher. Getting kindergartners to write through a computer is difficult at best. After a brainstorming session with Jon and Jenn, though, we came up with the first version of emoji writing for kindergarten.

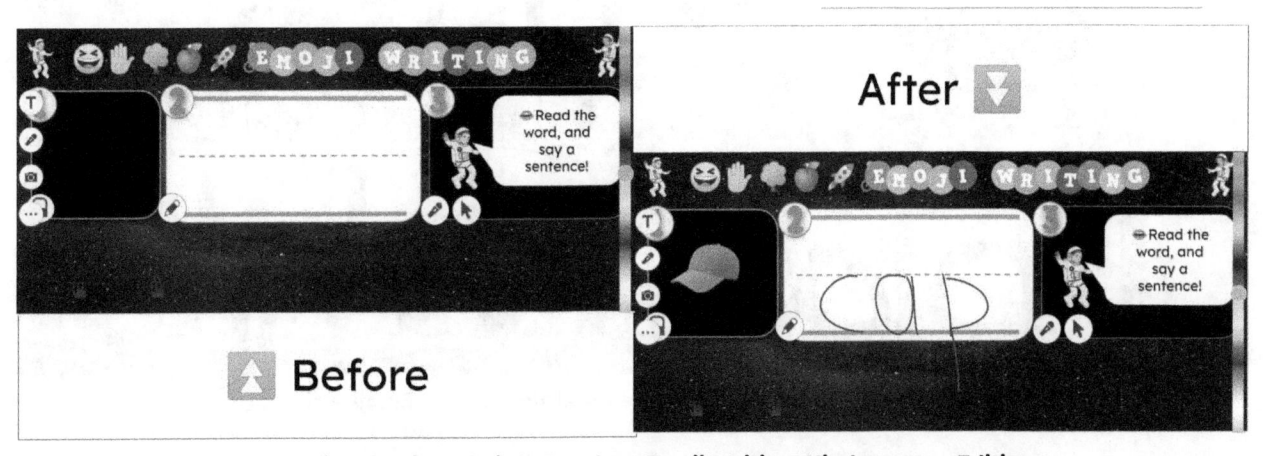

The first version of Little Random Emoji Writing: Kindergarten Edition.

Ben

This is a pretty simple template. To make this activity in Seesaw, I simply copy and paste an emoji image in the black square. Emojipedia is a great website with tons of emojis. Then I take a pen in Seesaw, change the color to black, and color over the emoji. As far as background goes, I make mine in Google Slides.

You can download the background template here.

tinyurl.com/
emojibackground

This kindergarten variation of Random Emoji Writing starts simply. In Seesaw, students erase a black square to reveal the emoji hidden underneath. After that, students use their knowledge of sounds to write a word to represent the emoji. Finally, they record themselves saying the word, sound by sound, as well as a sentence about the word.

We always perform the first rep with emoji writing as a whole group. I reveal an emoji, we generate some words to represent the emoji, and I use my whiteboard to write down a word we choose together. We break apart the word, and then come up with sentences about each word. After each word is written on the whiteboard, we pause and complete the Seesaw page for that specific word. As the pages progress, I am doing less modeling for students, and they begin to work out the words on the whiteboard in pairs and then by themselves. Typically, I save one or two words per Seesaw activity for students to do by themselves.

The next step is sending students to complete the activity on their own. This forms their second rep with the same activity. I find students are more confident when they do the activity by themselves at this point because it is the second time around. They work through each of the words at their own pace. Finally, we come back together and reflect on some of the completed Seesaw activities.

A completed Seesaw page for Little Random Emoji Writing.

As the students become more comfortable with the EduProtocol, I vary it to match the their growth. For example, instead of them all writing the same word, like *cap*, students write any word they want (i.e., *hat, blue, baseball*). We have great discussions about the different words we write for the different emojis. This collective reflection then turns into the next step: students can write multiple words for one emoji.

With this template of three words, some students might say three different sentences, one for each word, while others might combine the words they used into one (or two) sentences. Some students just write one word and one sentence because that is where they are in the progression.

After practicing this EduProtocol as a class, and as individuals, this activity can also become a center activity. Students who are already familiar with the activity can also write several words on their own. Because of the repetition of practice and flexibility in representing the emoji, students don't say, "Teacher, what is this?" when they are unsure what an emoji is "meant" to signify because they can write whatever word they want to write.

After I ran this EduProtocol several times, eventually I started to combine it with other activities. Three days a week for our morning message, we started with an emoji of the day, followed by a mini MathRep. Students quickly became very fluent in this activity. You can find more about that later in this book, in chapter 13, which covers how to rack and stack EduProtocols.

Once they have become familiar with this EduProtocol, students will have fun writing. This activity is a great way to practice phonics and help students build vocabulary through recording in Seesaw. Plus, when your class is ready, you can even start writing sentences to go with the different emojis.

Preparation

1. Whether I'm using a Seesaw template or paper, I find it helpful to plan the emojis students will be using. In the beginning, I focus on emojis that can be interpreted as CVC words, like *dog, pig, cap, cat*. As the year moves on, I choose

Ben

Even though pandemic teaching was tough, it was a great excuse to try new things. I try to remember this in my everyday teaching to keep pushing myself, and my students, in different ways. Oftentimes, students will surprise you when you give them a chance.

Jenn

Did you catch what Ben just said? The protocol changes as students grow and learn, is naturally differentiated, and allows for student choice. There are many "right" answers, and students can be successful and gain confidence in writing.

Ben

With this activity, I learned to put in more pages than most students can finish. This provides some built-in differentiation for students. Some students will finish the whole activity, most will finish a majority of the activity, and some will do only a few pages. As long as students are working hard and doing their best, then everyone's a winner.

emojis that may match some of the blends we are working on, like shark, frog, and drum.

2. Get your Seesaw activity ready with your preplanned emojis. You can either add your own emojis to Seesaw (tinyurl.com/emojiben), or you can simply place them on a projected Google Slide and have students write from there.

Updating and hiding an emoji in a Seesaw template

Ben

When/if students are ready, you can grab some primary paper, draw an emoji, and then have students write their own sentence(s) to go with the emoji. Students love drawing the emojis and are much more motivated to write as well. Students can bump it up by sharing with partners as they read their sentences.

Instructions

1. Prepare your Emoji Writing Seesaw activity on your computer. I use the sample, or demo, student to bring up the activity. In the beginning, I have students sit on the carpet and use whiteboards to follow along.

2. Have students get their "magic eraser" out. This is just the eraser tool in Seesaw. I slowly erase the emoji so that the students can guess what the emoji is, revealing it one dot, or click, at a time.

3. Discuss the different word(s) that could be used to represent the emoji. This is a great time for students to turn to their partners. As we are discussing the different words, we take time to break the words apart, count syllables, and iden-

tify beginning, middle, and ending sounds. I like to focus my time on whatever skill my students currently need.

4. Depending on the time of year, we will either write the word together, sound by sound, or students will try to write the whole word by themselves. We usually do this on whiteboards, but sometimes we use sound boxes to map out sounds. When we are done, we can share our word with the class or with a partner.

5. Once we have practiced writing a given word, it is time to come up with our own sentences to go along with it. We do our best to encourage fun and creative sentences. Students can brainstorm with a partner, but I encourage students to write the sentence on their whiteboard if they can.

6. Complete the Seesaw page. At this point, I choose one of the words from students to write on the page. Once the word is written, I will then record. To add some extra fun, I will move the emoji around and use it to sound out the word and then say a fun sentence. Another option is using a touch screen device and having the student come up and fill out the Seesaw template.

7. Repeat the steps above with a few more words. I often monitor the class's engagement to determine how many words to do together. I usually leave one or two at the end of the activity that we haven't done together to use as an assessment to see how the students are doing.

8. Release students to complete this activity on Seesaw. As students are completing the activity, walk around the room to help them. If you have a large group of students who still need help, pull the students into a small group and do the activity together on Seesaw.

9. If there is time, you can bring the students back to the carpet to check for completion in Seesaw, review how the students did, and even point out examples of awesomeness.

Marlena

Reinforcing strategies across your curriculum (like introducing a drum emoji when you are working on the *dr* blend) is gold. When all strategies reinforce the main curricular goal, students learn faster—it's just more reps with that skill!

Ben

One great feature in Seesaw is that a sample student can be included in your class. This allows you to use this sample student to demo or model activities with your class. You can use the present to class feature to model as well.

Ben

Sometimes kids have trouble making three boxes on primary paper. I introduce this by having students put their hands in the middle and draw a line on each side. It is quick and easy and mostly avoids those squishy boxes.

Jenn

I like to switch it up so they are constantly collaborating with different kids from the class. This is a great way to encourage team building and ensure that all students can learn and work together.

Jenn's Way (1st-2nd)

Getting students to write can sometimes feel intimidating in the TK-2 classroom, so I like to start teaching writing using the Random Emoji Paragraph. It makes the writing experience less intimidating and more fun!

Although I love technology, I also love using paper for specific EduProtocols, depending on the purpose of the protocol. Additionally, as a TK-2 teacher, I think it is extremely important to build fine motor skills, and using good old-fashioned paper and pencil can really help. I am also a firm believer in giving students time to think. So often, kids do not get that time, and that is why they do not answer. When given the time, they can really show us some amazing things. Doing it on paper helps this.

Students divide the drawing box with two vertical lines to create a space for the three emojis.

The first several times I do this EduProtocol, I want to be sure to model the process. I begin by having several students share their ideas. Together, we then combine our ideas to start our story. I write their answers on the whiteboard. Then we work together as a class to combine the ideas to make one expanded sentence. I do this because I think it models the collaboration. Our TK-2 students are still learning to be humans, and part of teaching the EduProtocols includes teaching them how to collaborate. Collaboration happens by sharing, thinking, and being willing to make compromises and come to an agreement. Using this strategy when I introduce the protocol also helps teach the collaboration aspect.

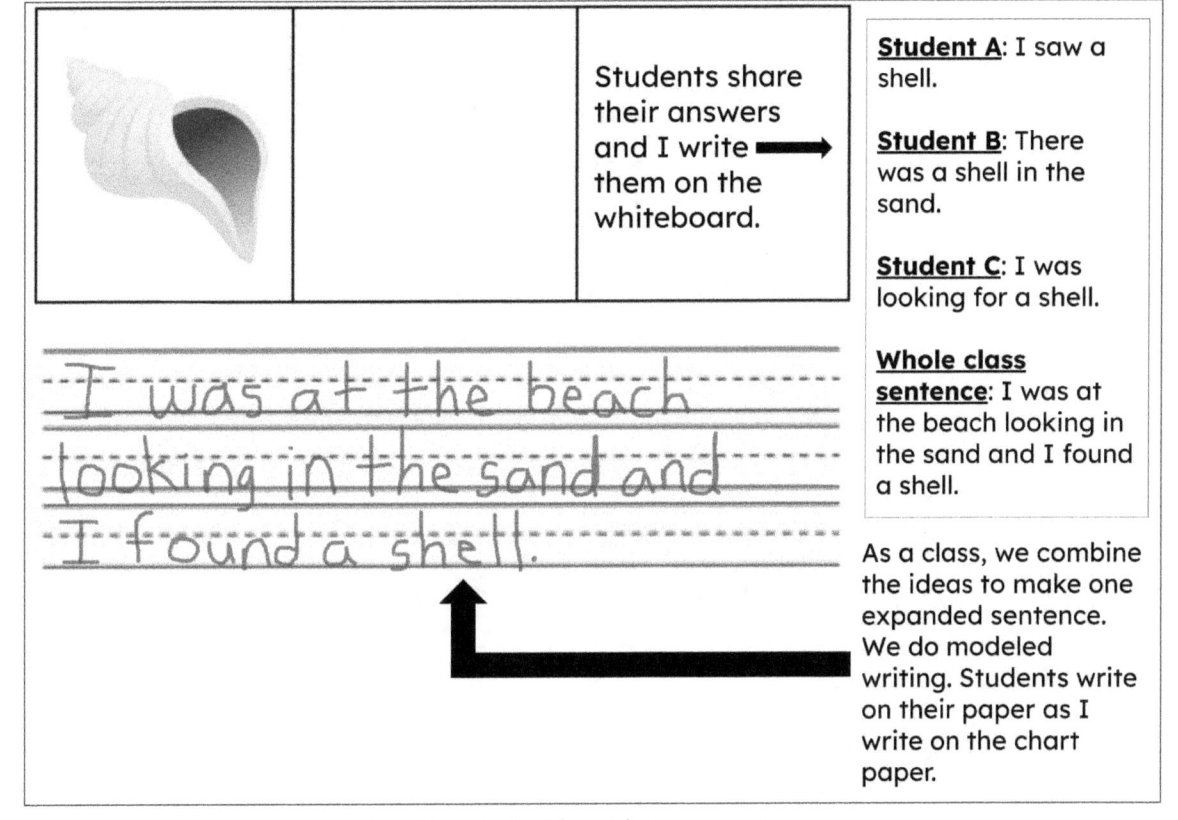

		Students share their answers and I write ➡ them on the whiteboard.	**Student A**: I saw a shell.
			Student B: There was a shell in the sand.
			Student C: I was looking for a shell.
I was at the beach looking in the sand and I found a shell. ⬆			**Whole class sentence**: I was at the beach looking in the sand and I found a shell.
			As a class, we combine the ideas to make one expanded sentence. We do modeled writing. Students write on their paper as I write on the chart paper.

Combine student input into one sentence.

Once we have collaborated and created our first sentence in our story, we model the writing. It is great to ask them how we start the sentence by using an uppercase letter, using finger spaces in between words, and sounding out words to spell. The more we model with active participation, the more the students try when we transition to independent writing with this same EduProtocol.

Ben

Jenn hits the nail on the head here with her connection to creativity. This is the same reason why in kindergarten we try to use different words to represent the same emoji. It helps kids develop flexible thinking and, of course, neurons.

> As I was playing with my new shell I realized it was an egg! It started to hatch a baby chicken! I got on my bike with the chicken and rode as fast as I could to the farm where he could live happily.

Student writing sample using emojis to spark the creativity

Ben

Jenn makes some great points here regarding feedback. With kindergarten students, the feedback process is much the same, but we are focusing on giving different items. I tend to focus on sounds, letter formation, and meaningful sentences. What's the same about both? Immediate feedback.

Each time I do this activity, I model it less and less. Instead, I ask students to direct me about what to do. This is when I know they are ready to work with partners. When I assign this EduProtocol to them as partners and as they are working, I facilitate by walking around the room and listening, or asking students questions to get them collaborating. I may also remind students about their writing conventions and teach in the moment, giving students immediate feedback. The more we do this, the less facilitating needs to happen and the better students get at writing and collaborating. What is the best part? If we do not do this EduProtocol once a week, students start asking me if we can do this. That's right—they're literally asking to write!

Another one of my favorite things about this protocol is how adaptable it is. If we really need to work on narrative writing, then we use the Random Emoji Power Paragraph to focus on narrative. Need to work on informational writing? Then whatever emoji pops up can be the topic to research. For example, let's say the first emoji is a snake. That means students will be writing an informational paragraph about snakes. The first sentence can be their introduction to the topic. The next emoji is an ice cream cone. To relate it to the topic of snakes, students can add information about food snakes eat. Continue for at least three emojis to get a strong informational paragraph.

> **Jenn**
>
> When doing this protocol, does one emoji equal one sentence? It doesn't have to! In this example, when the snake pops up, it can be one topic sentence, or it can be two or three sentences. There is not a rule for that!

Random Emoji 1 landed on a snake. This can be the main topic of the informational paragraph.

Random Emoji 2 landed on a bowl of ice cream. This can help give a detail. What does the snake eat?

Random Emoji 3 landed on a tree. This can help give another detail. Where does the snake live? What does its habitat look like?

Using the Random Emoji Generator for Informational Writing

The best part of using this protocol for informational writing is that students start to think creatively about research. Each time an emoji pops up, students wonder what they can research about the topic to make it connect. This makes their informational writing more creative and interesting and helps students to avoid writing thirty paragraphs that are basically the same.

Narrative and informational writing are two phenomenal ways to use this protocol, but there are even more options. What about opinion/persuasive writing? Why not generate an emoji and let that be

> **Jenn**
>
> Shh, it's a secret, but the Random Emoji Power Paragraph doesn't always have to be a paragraph! You can use it for writing different types of sentences, focusing on specific genres, and so much more.

the topic of persuasion? Did the emoji land on a bike? Students could write a persuasive essay on why biking is the best activity or why it is important to wear a helmet. You could also generate multiple emojis and let students choose which one they want to write an opinion/persuasive piece on.

In second-grade classrooms, I love using this EduProtocol for poetry. The first emoji becomes the main idea of the poem. Each additional emoji must be connected to the main idea.

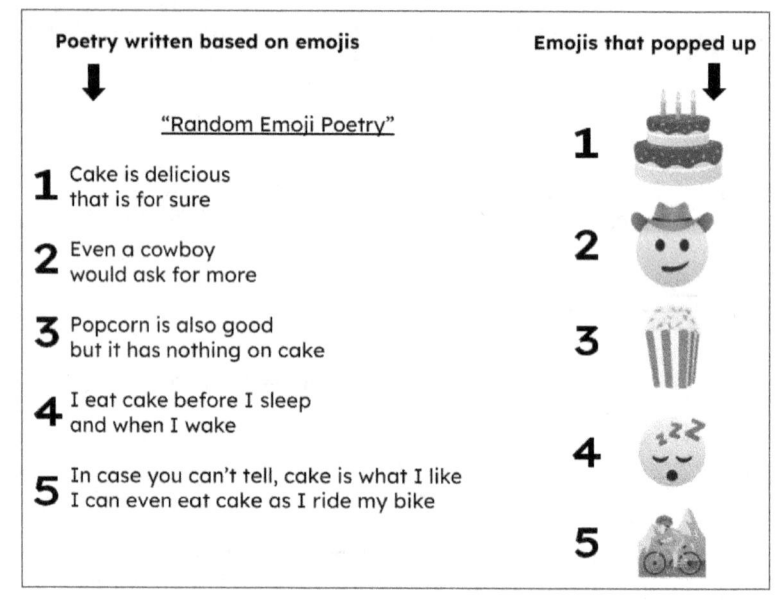

Poetry written based on emojis	Emojis that popped up
"Random Emoji Poetry"	
1 Cake is delicious that is for sure	1 🎂
2 Even a cowboy would ask for more	2 🤠
3 Popcorn is also good but it has nothing on cake	3 🍿
4 I eat cake before I sleep and when I wake	4 😴
5 In case you can't tell, cake is what I like I can even eat cake as I ride my bike	5 🚴

Using the Random Emoji Generator for Writing Poetry

As we practice this EduProtocol more, I can choose to have the emojis pre-generated, or I can use the random emoji generator Jon and Marlena created at eduprotocols.com/class. The process is the same, except the generator will reveal one emoji at a time. What is really awesome about the tool are the different modes. There is a Pure Random mode and also a Storymoji mode. Additionally, you can choose to animate the emojis!

Another helpful part of using this tool is that if an emoji shows up that is too hard to relate to the story or topic, you can click on the emoji and spin again to generate a new one. Whether you pre-generate the emojis or use the truly random emoji generator, your students will learn how to be creative writers, have fun, and ask you to write paragraphs.

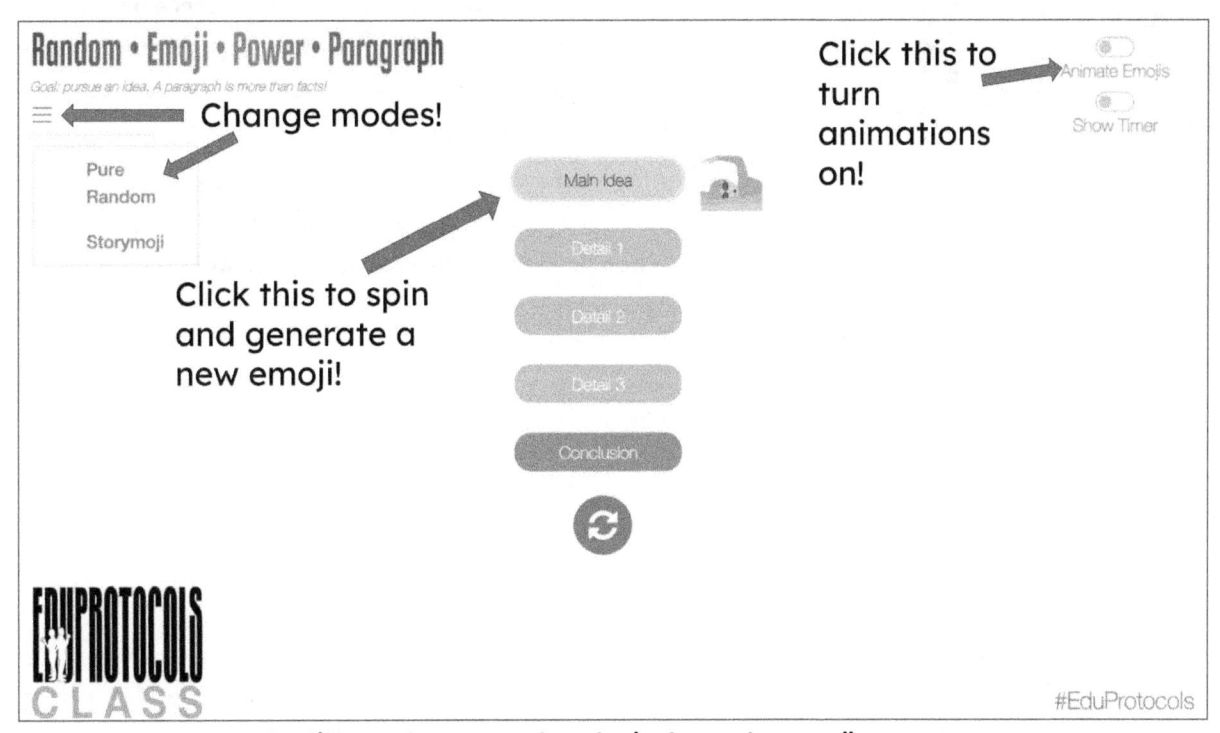

The different features and modes in the random emoji generator.

Preparation

1. Decide how you want to perform this activity. Are you going to use paper? Google Slides? Seesaw? Set that up (have writing journals, or assign a template in Google/Seesaw).

2. Pull up the random emoji generator (eduprotocols.com/class). Or choose the emojis ahead of time and have them preloaded on an activity. That's it! You are prepared!

Instructions

1. Show the first emoji. Have students start their story using the emoji. As they are writing, walk around and give immediate feedback on writing.

> **Ben & Jenn**
>
> One reason we highly recommend Seesaw is the ability to add voice to writing. By simply having students use the microphone to record themselves reading their writing, you are helping them master so many standards, including many ELD standards.

2. Show the next emoji. Have students add to their story using the emoji. Remember: the key is that they are adding to their story and not writing a different sentence that is completely unrelated. As they are writing, walk around and give immediate feedback on writing. Continue this for as many emojis as you want to use.

3. When students are done writing, have them share their stories with a partner. Or, if you are performing the EduProtocol in Google Slides or Seesaw, have students look over others' writing right away.

Extended Content:
Little Random Emoji Writing

Little Random Emoji Writing can be a ton of fun using the EduProtocols Emoji Generator, but you can also adapt it to use in Seesaw as well.

In the extended content, you'll get:
- ★ Tips and tricks to adapt this protocol to use in Seesaw
- ★ To learn how to edit and create templates for Emoji Writing in Seesaw
- ★ Access to Seesaw templates/activities ready to use today
- ★ Templates, resources, student examples, and more

My notes:

How It Looks in Seesaw	Templates & Resources	Student Examples
tinyurl.com/EmojiSeesaw Password: 73468	tinyurl.com/EmojiFolder	tinyurl.com/EmojiExamples

Chapter 10
Fast and Curious EduProtocol

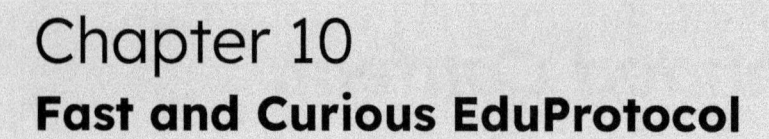

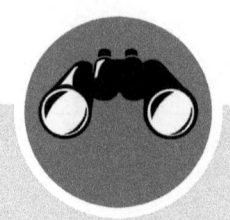

It is easy to look at a quiz tool and see it only as an assessment tool, but with Fast and Curious (FAC), we are going to challenge your thinking about how a quiz program can become first instruction instead of the last assessment. FAC can shift a quiz program from assessment to instructional tool due to two tiny factors.

First, Fast and Curious provides an immediate second chance and involves whole-class progress. In the traditional FAC format, teachers provide an opportunity for students to take a quiz, the whole class quickly reviews the answers, and then students immediately retake the quiz. This forces students to immediately recall what they just reviewed before the answers fade from memory. Repeated over a few days, the results can be remarkable!

Fast and Curious's second tiny shift is that the EduProtocol focuses less on individual progress (Yes, we really said that!) and more on whole-class progress. This sets students up for a growth mindset approach and makes space for everyone to feel good about their contribution, and when we feel good, we try harder—much harder!

> **Marlena**
>
> We see students (the ones you would least suspect of doing do) begging to take quizzes home for extra practice just so they can do better in class. And nobody actually looks at their individual scores . . . but they keep track!

Academic Goals

- Students build fluency in subject matter
- Provides students with quick repetition of concepts
- Focuses on one skill/standard to practice

Teacher Big Ideas

- Students get immediate feedback.

- Activity can be easily differentiated for students.
- Builds fluency into mastery.
- Teacher has immediate access to data-driven instruction.
- Easy and fast assessment = saves teacher time/sanity.

Original EduProtocol: Fast and Curious

Fast and Curious was originally designed as an entry-level vocabulary activity. Since its inception, it has morphed to include many other topics like math facts, sight words, sounds—anything that requires fluency. FAC should be conducted daily over the course of a school week.

1. The first step is to design your quiz in your app of choice, or find one that's already made. We prefer Quizizz, but there are many great apps out there to choose from (i.e., Gimkit, Blooket, Wordwall, 99Math, and more). Remember to limit the number of questions to how long you want the quiz to take. We suggest 5–10 questions for speed.
2. On day one, students come in and take a pretest.
3. Review the data with students, focusing on rapid review of the three or four most missed questions.
4. Then, immediately, students do another rep, literally the same activity they just did.
5. Repeat this process over a few days, focusing on the words or items students miss after each repetition.
6. By day four, your whole class score should be awesome (typically maintaining a class average above 90 percent), but if not, you can repeat another round and try again on day five. If your scores from day four rock, you have earned yourself an extra day and extra time for something else.

Jenn
You don't have to use the same tool every time. Find one you like and use it. Then, if you want to try another one, do it! In fact, I use different tools for different purposes.

Jon
A major advantage with Blooket, Gimkit, and Wordwall is that students can play as much as they like, not just once. Instead of 10–12 questions in a session, kids might do 25–30. I've seen this happen in groups of up to 100 first graders at once. It's electric.

Marlena
Focus on first instruction, not first assessment.

Marlena
Spaced practice (practice over time) is more effective for learning content than mass (cramming) practice.

> **Marlena**
>
> FAC in kindergarten may be very different than FAC in first or second grade, as the attention span of kindergartners is still developing.

Ben's Way (Kindergarten)

As a kindergarten teacher, I feel that everything takes longer for students to do. That said, as the year progresses, I find that my students can do Fast and Curious fairly quickly. With this in mind, I sometimes deploy this protocol a little differently.

First of all, instead of trying to give a quiz four to five times a week for one week, I may repeat the quiz three times a week over two weeks. Instead of cycling through two quizzes each day, I want to reinforce learning over a period of time, rather than taking a random guess-and-check approach. There are a few ways that I execute FAC.

- **As an Opening Activity:** A great way to start a quiz is when students first come into class. I use this as their morning work for some weeks because kids come in with their computers in their hands. It all depends on how students are doing and their attention span at the moment. I may review the data afterward.

- **As a Carpet Time Activity:** Sometimes I do the quiz as a whole-class carpet time activity. We review the correct answers, and then students either do the quiz again on their own or do it the next morning; it all depends on how long it takes and their attention span at the time.

- **For Early Finishers:** I also make FAC quizzes available as early finisher activities. That way students can practice on their own. Most quiz tools have an asynchronous or homework mode that allows students to take quizzes on their own time. As students gain more reps, I gather data on difficult questions or students who need more support. I find this data great for determining small groups, as it is readily available.

- **As Formative Assessment:** If I don't review the quiz answers with students, I look at quiz data later, and I use students' progress as a formative assessment to guide my teaching. If many students aced the quiz, it's the perfect time to move into small-group instruction.

- **As a Summative Assessment:** Lastly, as educators, we know assessment is huge for driving our instruction. Remember pulling students one by one to assess them? In a class of thirty kindergartners, individual assessments on letter and sound recognition can take weeks to complete, only for the data to be different by the end of the assessment because now students may know more than they did three weeks ago. While FAC is not an assessment strategy, once my kindergartners become familiar with the quiz program we are using, it becomes easier to use this tool purely for assessment from time to time. There is nothing wrong with that!

> **Ben**
>
> It is super important to take the time to help students identify when they get an answer correct, and when an answer is incorrect. We can't assume students will automatically understand the feedback the computer is giving them.

I take many things into consideration when building my quizzes. My first thought is, does this skill or concept fit into Fast and Curious mode? As mentioned above, I find that skills that require fluency are good for this protocol (i.e., math facts, sounds, letter names, sight words, and even CVC words).

Next, I consider what time of the year it is. At the beginning of the year, I tend to offer fewer choices and fewer questions for students. As students learn the program and become more fluent, I add answer choices and increase the number of questions. For my first quiz, I may start with only two-answer choices. For my next interaction, I make a copy of the quiz and add a third. I may even make another copy and add more answer choices, depending on how the students are doing.

A progression of options in Fast and Curious as students gain confidence.

Easier quiz question vs. a more difficult quiz question that requires more reading.

In line with answer choices, I think it is important to think about how questions are built for Fast and Curious. For example, if I have a student practice CVC words toward the beginning of the year, I might put a CVC word, like *cat*, as the question and then use a few different images as an answer. As students become more fluent with the CVC words, I may move the image to the question and have the words as images. Notice that in the first example students are reading one word, while in the second example, students are reading three words.

Another item to consider is how many questions you want to include. Typically for FAC, I want students to get about 5-10 minutes of practice time. I have tried to run FAC with all the sounds of the alphabet, but the quiz took too long, and some students got bored or frustrated. Instead, I find it better to start by giving the whole alphabet only one time, and then focus on five to ten items that students have the most difficulty with. Once students have mastered those five to ten, I can move on to the next chunk.

Now with all of these things rattling around in my brain, I am ready to build, or find someone else's, quiz in my app of choice.

Instructions

1. Getting Started: Start the quiz. To distribute the quiz, I copy and paste the link into Seesaw; that way, students can find it easily and I can distribute it quickly.

Ben

Some programs have a preview or practice mode in which students don't need to enter their name. I like to use this mode at the beginning of the year because it makes it easier for students. The downside of this is that I don't have access to student data. An upside is that students get practice with the concept and with the program.

Ben

Even though it takes more time, I usually end up building my own quiz. This way, I can really make sure it matches my students' learning needs, curriculum, etc. Over the years, I have built up a collection of quizzes that suits my students' needs.

2. **Pre-Rep:** Typically for our first rep on a new quiz, we do the quiz all together on the carpet. I either use my computer hooked up to the display or I will hook up a student computer. I remind students how to find the quiz on their computer, what buttons to push, and where to type their name. Sometimes, I will control the computer and select the answers, or sometimes, I will hook up a touch screen Chromebook to my projector/TV and choose individual students to answer the questions. In both methods, the students on the carpet can participate by indicating their answer with fingers or a whiteboard.

3. **Rep 1:** After we have completed the pre-rep, students get their Chromebooks and try the test for the first time. I usually don't review incorrect answers on the first day, but I do look at the data and try to pull those students who need more support in the concept during small-group instruction. Our main goal for the first time doing a specific quiz is to just become familiar with the words and concepts of the quiz so that students can work through the quiz the next time more fluently and on their own.

4. **Rep 2:** As I mentioned above, I sometimes run this protocol three times a week for two weeks, but sometimes I will run it every day for one week; it really depends on what else I have going on. Students will take this quiz, and after the quiz is over, I will review the answers that the class struggled with the most. If I have time, I will run the quiz again.

5. **Reps 3, 4, and 5:** Run these reps the same way as rep 2. I look at student progress to see who needs more support and who has mastered the concept. If students have mastered the quiz concepts, I sometimes give them the choice of another activity or another quiz that may be slightly longer or harder. With students who need more support, I typically try to offer more small-group support, which gives those students access to the material in a different way.

6. **Last Rep (usually 5 or 6):** Usually by rep 6, a majority of the class has mastered the concept. If it is the first five to ten

> Try Ben's quizzes in Quizizz and Seesaw!
>
> tinyurl.com/QuizizzBen

> **Ben**
> Sometime at the beginning of the year, I will send the quiz home to parents in a message. That way students can get exposed to the app with some one-on-one help before we use it in the classroom.

> **Ben**
> Calling students to come up and select answers is a great incentive for students. I let them know I will only select them if they are engaged in their learning. Sometimes, I will let students select the next person.

sounds of the alphabet, I can now move on to the next five to ten sounds. At this point, I may still have a small group of students who have not mastered the skill, so those students continue to receive small-group support.

Jenn's Way (1st-2nd)

Fast and Curious is the EduProtocol I start with. Just as the name says, it's fast! It engages the students in the learning process, and they immediately start seeing their growth.

In my class, I really like to focus on team building, so for me this EduProtocol is all about growing as a team. One of my favorite ways to introduce Fast and Curious is with student names and pictures (see chapter 14 for more info). I always start by playing a live session. However, as the year progresses, I love to start using Fast and Curious as a center activity. So as the students master the protocol, this gets to morph into their independent practice as a center! Students work on FAC over time, and at their own pace, as they "pass" multiple levels.

Preparation

To prepare for the activity, all you have to do is think, "What is the skill I want my students to master?" Or, "What is the skill I want to assess?" For me, I use this a lot with math fluency, vocabulary acquisition, sight words, and MathReps (more on that in chapter 11).

So let's say you want to teach the vocabulary for your ELA unit. In that case, you have to do the following steps.

1. Find a digital online assessment tool (like Quizizz) that covers the skill you are wanting to teach/master. You can also make your own, but there are millions, so save yourself the time.

2. Add that quiz to your library so you can play it with your students. Now you have prepared for the activity. It's that simple! Time to implement it.

Ben

If we are using a tool or a mode that shows class average, I think it is important to remind students about the class average. You can write those scores on a whiteboard or chart paper to monitor growth as a class.

Jon

It is easy to differentiate with two quizzes for one class. Just open another browser window and have two games going at the same time! One game can be "entry level" and the other can be "expert round." I aim to get everyone into the expert round by the third or fourth try.

Jon

If you use Gimkit, you can set the time so the whole class practices for a solid three to four minutes, then everyone stops together. Do a quick review, and then everyone tries again in the next three-to-four-minute sprint. That's the Fast and Curious!

Chapter 10 | Fast and Curious EduProtocol | 95

Instructions

1. If you're using Quizizz, click "Start live quiz" for the quiz you want to use.
2. Have students join the activity.
3. Rep 1: Students play and see their score.
4. At the end of the first round, write down the overall class proficiency on the board so they can track it.
5. Quickly look at the data. What questions need to be taught, and what questions don't? Quickly teach. In this example, teach the vocabulary.

Jenn

For Quizizz, click "Start live quiz" ahead of time, and then click the link icon to copy the link. Post the link in Seesaw, Google Classroom, or Canvas so students can click the link and get to the activity without entering any join codes. This will save so much time! Some students can enter that join code really quickly, and for others it is much harder. Using the "copy link" feature ensures easy accessibility by all students.

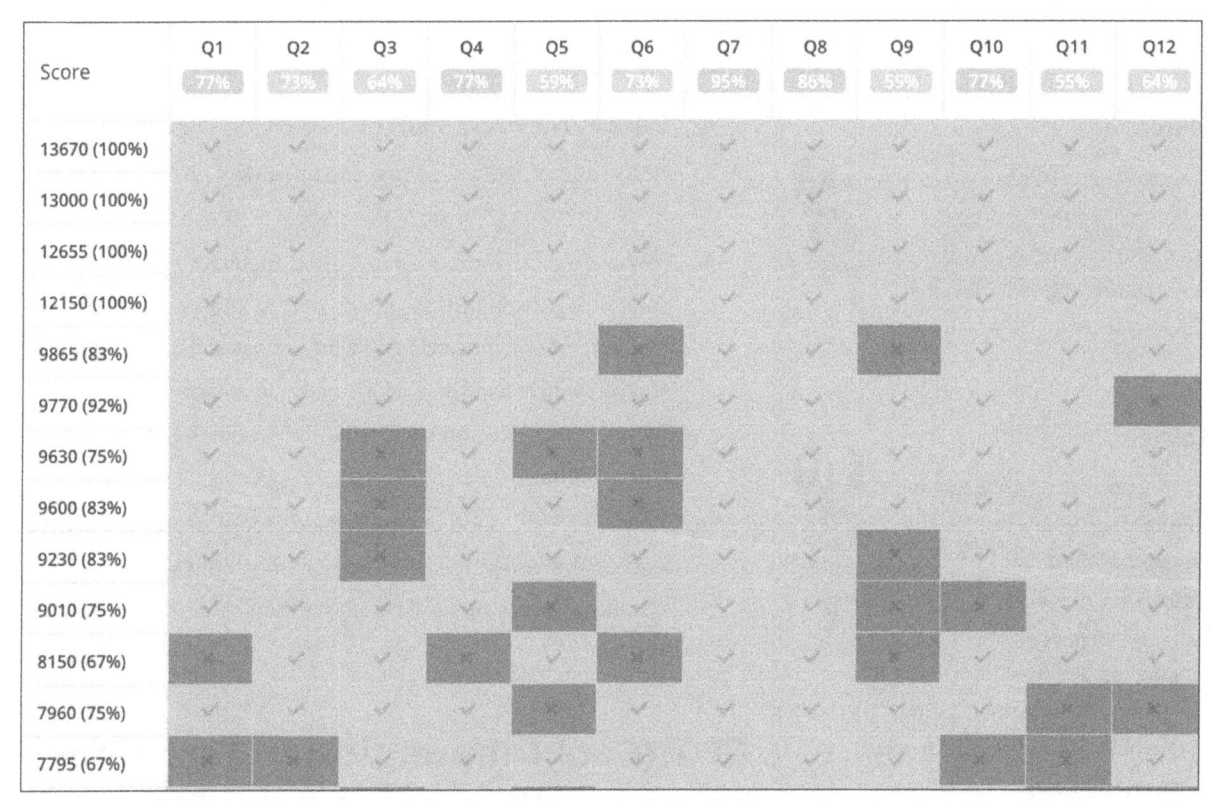

Score	Q1 77%	Q2 73%	Q3 64%	Q4 77%	Q5 59%	Q6 73%	Q7 95%	Q8 86%	Q9 55%	Q10 77%	Q11 55%	Q12 64%
13670 (100%)	✓	✓	✓	✓	✓	✓	✓	✓	✓	✓	✓	✓
13000 (100%)	✓	✓	✓	✓	✓	✓	✓	✓	✓	✓	✓	✓
12655 (100%)	✓	✓	✓	✓	✓	✓	✓	✓	✓	✓	✓	✓
12150 (100%)	✓	✓	✓	✓	✓	✓	✓	✓	✓	✓	✓	✓
9865 (83%)	✓	✓	✓	✓	✓	✗	✓	✓	✗	✓	✓	✓
9770 (92%)	✓	✓	✓	✓	✓	✓	✓	✓	✓	✓	✓	✗
9630 (75%)	✓	✓	✗	✓	✗	✗	✓	✓	✓	✓	✓	✓
9600 (83%)	✓	✓	✗	✓	✓	✗	✓	✓	✓	✓	✓	✓
9230 (83%)	✓	✓	✓	✓	✓	✓	✓	✓	✗	✗	✓	✓
9010 (75%)	✓	✓	✓	✓	✗	✗	✓	✓	✗	✗	✓	✓
8150 (67%)	✗	✓	✓	✓	✗	✗	✓	✗	✓	✓	✓	✓
7960 (75%)	✓	✓	✓	✓	✗	✗	✓	✓	✓	✓	✗	✗
7795 (67%)	✗	✗	✓	✓	✓	✓	✓	✓	✓	✗	✓	✓

Take a quick look at student responses to decide which questions need more review.

Level up your quizzes by assigning more than one quiz at a time!

> **Jenn**
>
> Teaching students how to enter join codes is another skill that you can easily do later in first grade and all the time in second grade.

> **Jenn**
>
> If the class as a whole scores higher than 90 percent on the second or third rep, I usually stop. They've mastered it, and we can move on to something else. However, for the students who may need a little more help, we do the fourth and fifth rep as a small group. This way, as a class, we are still growing in another area, but I am helping ALL students master the standards.

6. Rep 2: Play the quiz again and watch the score go up!
7. At the end of the quiz, write down the new proficiency score. Show students their growth.
8. Review the answers quickly, with a focus on the correct answer. Keep explanations short and to the point. Then play again to see if they can beat their class score. The point of this is to increase their score as a class, not necessarily as individuals. Focusing on team building and becoming stronger together.
9. Reps 3–5: Play another day to beat the score again. By the end of the week, the students will not only know their vocabulary words but will be using them correctly in context for fun!

CDT (Cool Differentiation Technique) Alert!

One of our favorite ways to run Fast and Curious is as a self-paced activity. This involves opening two or more quizzes at a time (each one more challenging than the other or with progressive concepts). When kids pass the first level, they can move to the more advanced activity! You can embed the links to the different quizzes into an activity or slide. Then, let students choose which quiz they are ready for, or give a strong recommendation on which level they should start with.

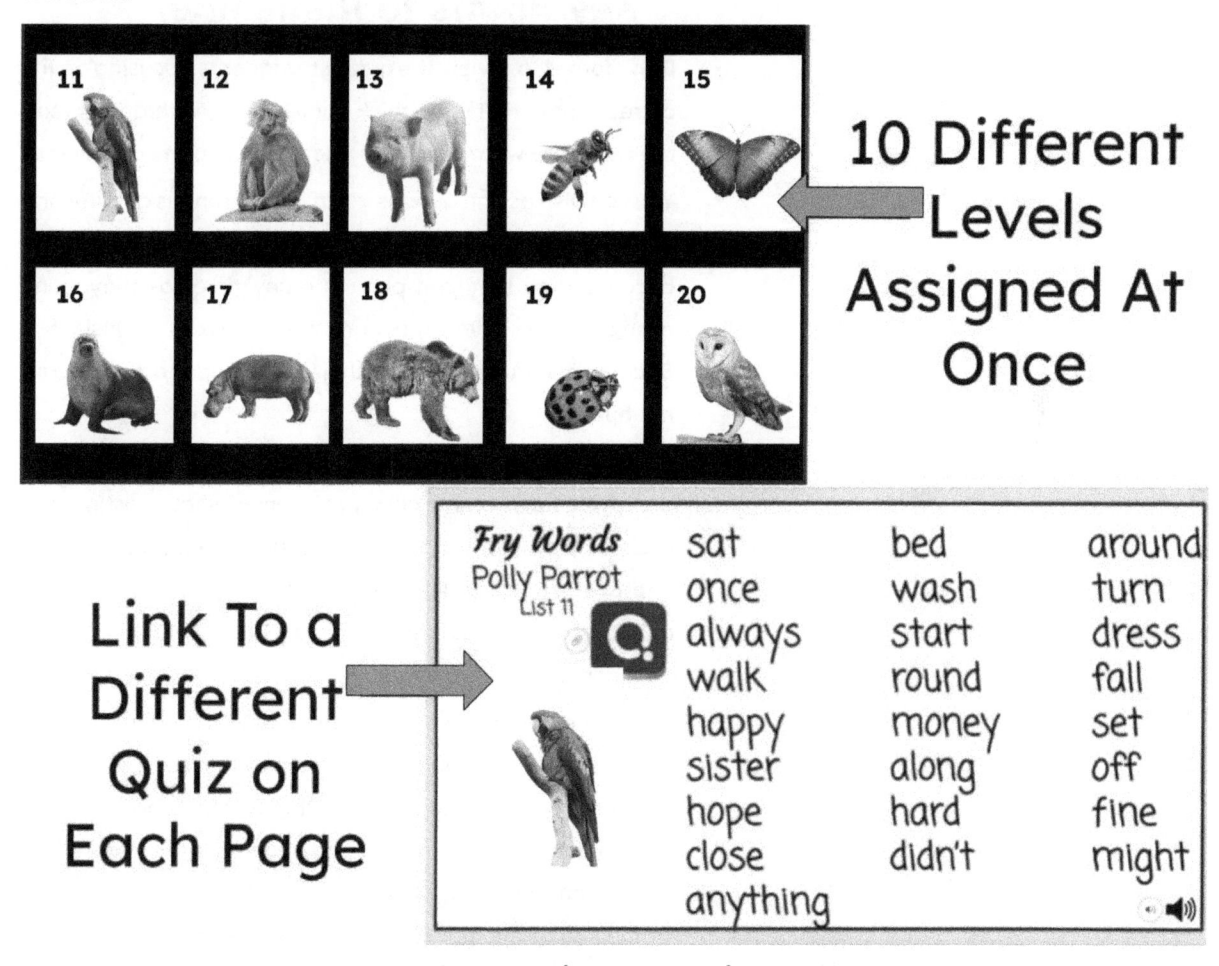

A sample progression through quizzes by level

If you want, you can really get fancy by offering a cornucopia of quizzes. For example, we run a set of ten or more quizzes for sight words, where every quiz is the next set of twenty-five sight words. Students can progressively move through the levels of words as they learn each set. You can keep track of student progress or let students track their own growth and play at their own pace!

One of the reasons we really love this student-paced model is that it allows for a ton of differentiation for all students. Check out chapter 13, about stacking EduProtocols, for more ideas around how to differentiate FAC.

Key Points to Remember

- Don't forget to review the quiz with students, focusing on the correct answers. These quick mini-lessons, with an immediate retry, are what take Fast and Curious to the next level.

- You can also assign quizzes as an asynchronous activity or a homework assignment. Students often ask for this approach because then they can play as many times as they want, even at home. Believe it or not, students ask to do this! Why? Because they want to beat their score and more reps cannot hurt.

- Focus on improving as a class. When looking at the data you are given, focus on the class proficiency, what questions the class as a whole had the most difficulty with, and how to improve as a class. Focusing on individual scores for your own personal assessment is great, but not for the actual Fast and Curious protocol.

- Take time to discuss with students how to internalize the feedback given by the program. Ensure the test shows which answer is correct after the question is answered. Point out to students what this means, and make sure they look at the correct answer. Also, some quizzes will review the answers at the end of the quiz. Stop and show students how to navigate this feature and what it means!

- Use Fast and Curious for centers! Once kids get proficient in the protocol, you can use this as one of your centers. This allows students more time to practice, builds more time into other areas of your schedule, and is an easy center to prep. This is a great tool for differentiation because you can assign different levels of quizzes for different groups of students.

What We Look for in a Quiz App

There are so many great tools out there to use for Fast and Curious, but we want to look for certain features in an app to help our pre-readers succeed. Here are some functions we look for when we choose a tool for FAC.

- Link Sharing: Do students have to type in a code, or can I share a link with students that will take them directly to the quiz? Being able to copy and paste a link to share with students makes it much easier for students to get inside the quiz.

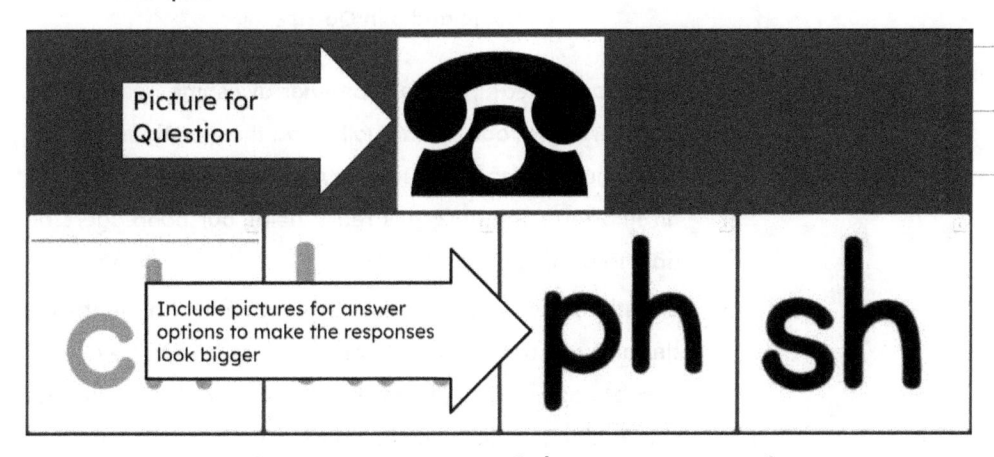

Make sure your response choices are easy to read.

- Pictures/Images: Does the app let you add a picture/image as a question? Does it let you add the picture/image as an answer? We love tools that do both. It is super useful when matching words, letters, or numbers with different pictures. Also using pictures for responses sometimes helps the text appear much bigger than the default text in a program.
- Audio/Video Recording: Being able to record a question as a video is nice, but most importantly, we love apps that let us record our own audio. We can record ourselves reading sight words, or saying a sound or a number. For Smart Start FAC, when students are learning their friends' names, you can record students' names so they can match them with the image of their friend.

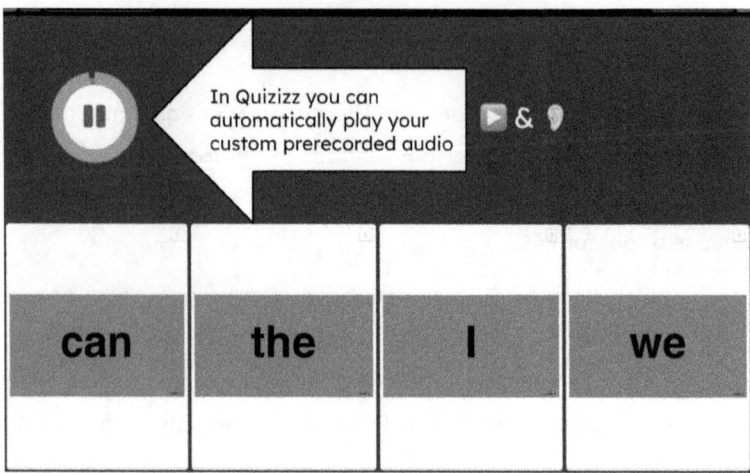

Using audio in Quizizz

- **Read to Me Feature:** This is another awesome accessibility feature. Some tools will actually read the questions and answers out loud to the students. Again, like adding audio or an image to the quiz, this really helps our nonreaders be able to participate in the FAC.
- **Question/Response Shuffling:** Being able to change the order of questions is great. Some students love to be able to look at each other's screens for the answers. When you can shuffle the questions and responses, this helps alleviate this problem. Furthermore, some students are really good at remembering specific question and answer locations. When the order of questions can change, this is a great help.
- **Premade Library:** What kind of premade quizzes are available? Is there a small selection, or do you have tons to choose from? Even if you end up making your own quiz, looking at a premade library can give you tons of ideas.

With this in mind, our favorite tool to use is Quizizz. It pretty much meets all these criteria. However, we also love 99Math, WordWall.net, and Blooket. Again it's not about the tool, but the pedagogy. So pick what works for you! Lastly, a quick PSA. It's always important to make sure your online tool meets student safety and privacy guidelines before using.

Extended Content:
Fast & Curious

Fast & Curious is a quick way to engage students in their learning. Giving students access to a quiz quickly is a must for this EduProtocol.

In the extended content, you'll get:
- ★ Tips on how to quickly allow students to access quizzes
- ★ Ideas on how to extend FAC to other times of the day
- ★ Templates, resources, and more

My notes:

How It Looks in Seesaw	Templates & Resources
tinyurl.com/FACSeesawEC Password: 73468	tinyurl.com/FACFolder

Chapter 11
MathReps EduProtocol

Ben & Jenn

If you haven't read *The Edu-Protocol Field Guide: Math Edition* by Lisa Nowakowski and Jeremiah Ruesch, you need to! It will help you take your MathReps game to the next level.

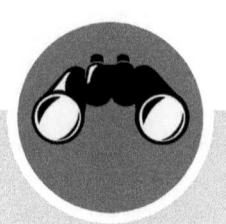

How many times have you heard parents say, "My child is not good at math"? How many times have you taught a mathematical concept in September and then, when it came for the spiral review, the students acted like they had never heard of that concept before?

This happens a lot, and it is because of the way our textbooks are structured: you teach a concept, and you move on. There might be a spiral review at the end or beginning of each chapter, but it is not consistent. We all know the saying "If you don't use it, you lose it," and that is exactly what happens in math. They do not see how mathematical concepts work together. This is very similar to what happens with parts of speech (see chapter 8 on Little p*ARTS).

The solution? In *The EduProtocol Field Guide, Math Edition*, Lisa Nowakowski came to the rescue and developed the amazing MathReps! In Lisa's words, "MathReps is an activity in which students take a number through a series of related concepts and standards at one time." Students then use a work mat to practice skills together. This process helps them to not just learn a concept but to truly master it and understand how math concepts work together.

Academic Goals

- Students master key math standards and concepts
- Students benefit from a spiral review of previously learned concepts
- Students level up through a progression of concepts as previous skills are mastered

Teacher Big Ideas

- Use MathReps as a warmup or to help access prior knowledge.
- Build MathReps across the year to master and practice different skills.
- Customize MathReps to meet the needs of your curriculum, standards, and students.

Original EduProtocol: MathReps

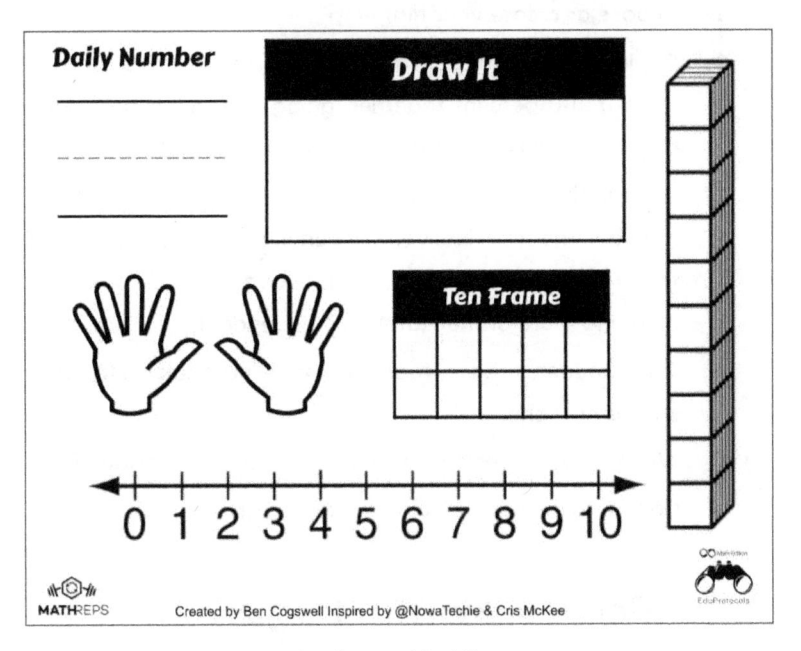

A primary MathRep

What's in a MathRep? MathReps were designed by Lisa Nowakowski for *The EduProtocol Field Guide: Math Edition* and were initially formulated as a math spin on another EduProtocol, 8 p*ARTS. As we know from chapter 8, in 8 p*ARTS, students practice and master many different parts of speech at one time. So Lisa took this same idea and applied it to math, and voila, MathReps were born.

MathReps are centered around a math mat, which is basically one piece of paper that targets multiple standards or skills. Some math mats focus on using one number, which you can manipulate in multiple ways. Other math mats may focus on the same skill with different numbers. With repetition and practice, students master each of the skills or standards, and because of the spiral nature of MathReps, students retain these skills over time.

Of course, not all these math mats are on paper. You can use Google Slides, Nearpod, or another great tool—you guessed it, Seesaw.

In the original MathReps, the EduProtocol followed these steps.

Steps

1. Choose or create your MathRep.
2. Deploy your MathRep. The first time you do this, you complete it 100 percent together, going over each part. Each day you do this, you can do less and less together.
3. Repeat the MathRep several times during the week. Remember, the first time you will heavily do the teaching of all the areas on the MathRep, but by day five, students should be doing more of the MathRep independently.
4. Once students have mastered that particular MathRep, start a new one.
5. When they master the new one, go back to the original.
6. Continue this pattern to continue the reps.

Ben's Way (Kindergarten)

When I first started teaching kindergarten, I was amazed by all the different types of graphic organizers and manipulatives students needed to use. The ten frames, number bonds, and number lines/paths were all swirling in my head. I knew I needed to prepare my students because they needed these tools as they moved up into the higher grades. Plus they seemed like great tools to support conceptual development in math. However, I found that as soon as I introduced a new tool, students would forget the previous one. Enter MathReps!

MathReps was one of the first EduProtocols I started implementing when I started teaching in kindergarten. At the time, I was work-

---

Lisa

No matter your preferred tool, the outcome will be the same: better understanding and mastery. I love how both Ben and Jenn have taken the concept of MathReps and run with it. Their adaptations have taken this simple concept to the next level.

Jon

High school students struggle with Number Sense and Math Facts. I've seen the power of MathReps in my sixth-grade class for remediation. What if we fixed the issue at the source?

Collection of Kindergarten MathReps

tinyurl.com/kindermathreps

ing with three other amazing kindergarten teachers, and I was the new kid on the block. They all knew that I loved technology, but not everyone was as comfortable with it as I was. Also, as far as pacing and curriculum, we were all at different points and different pages. However, when we started looking at Lisa's MathReps, everyone was interested, and we jumped in.

Inspired by a kindergarten MathRep by Lisa and Cris McKee, my team and I adapted what they had to match our curriculum and students' needs. After we came to a consensus, we hit the print button and ran that baby over to the copy machine, and the next day we were ready to roll.

After a few short weeks, our students were soaring through the concepts covered by our new MathRep, and those new ideas were sticking in their brains. As the year went on, so did the progression of the MathReps. And over the next few years, the progression has grown and become more refined. Here's a more current progression of MathReps. Keep in mind that even this progression keeps changing, so scan the QR code on page 104 for the most current kinder version or visit MathReps.com.

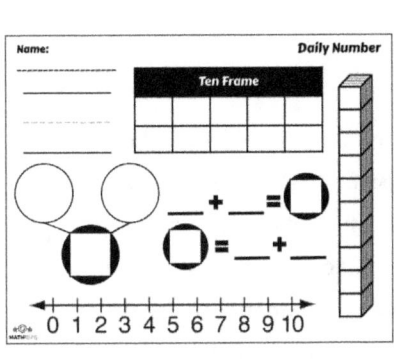

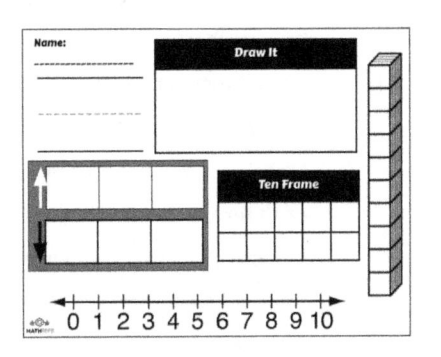

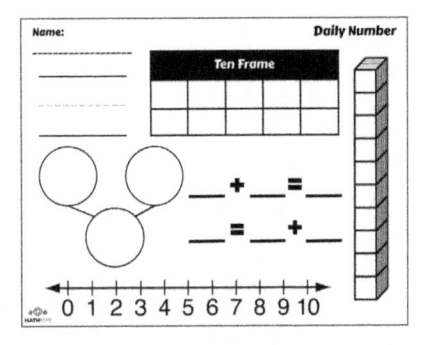

> **Jenn**
>
> Me too! MathReps was one of the very first I started with because I could really see how important it was. It was the EduProtocol that got me hooked and changed the way I taught.

> **Ben**
>
> I love this progression, but perhaps one of my favorite additions to MathReps was when I added a "build it" section. I simply added a square in the lower left-hand corner and wrote "build it" inside. In this section, students use their Unifix cubes to build the daily number, which makes their MathRep three-dimensional.

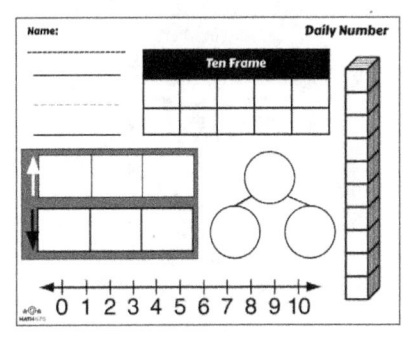

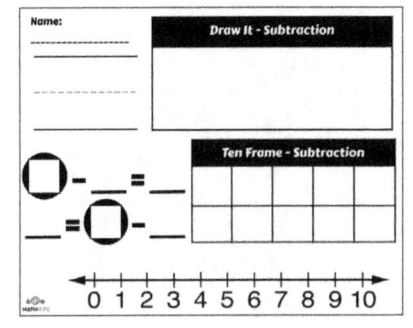

An example of a MathRep progression in Kindergarten

Jenn

Although these are what Ben uses in kindergarten, I use the same ones in first grade for the first month of school. The progression is great. It reinforces number sense to 10 and gets students used to MathReps. The only difference is, I start with the bottom row.

Ben

One of my favorite things about doing MathReps on the computer is that the keyboard has a number line built in.

For the most current MathReps, go to MathReps.com.

Ben's mini MathRep number booklet.

tinyurl.com/ mathrepbooklet

As you can see from the progression, each time the reps progress, only one of the components changes. Students take almost no time to adjust to the new section.

As we progress into addition, students can use two markers. The two different colors represent the two different addends that make the sum. For each different rep, the different colors need to match. For example, if there are four green dots in the ten frame, four Unifix cubes need to be colored green, four jumps on the number line are green, and the number 4 is always written in green. The same would be true of the other color. For students, this helps to reinforce that the sum or daily number can be made up of two other numbers.

As the years and students change, I always adjust my MathReps to meet the students' needs. Further, as students master the rep on paper, they can follow a similar format in Seesaw. (Check out How It Looks in Seesaw to learn more.)

Preparation

1. Choose or create your MathRep. Typically, we start MathReps on paper since it tends to be faster than using a computer. It is best to ensure students are familiar with all the skills before they start on the MathRep. Refer to your standards, curriculum, or students' needs. You can check out my current MathReps progression at tinyurl.com/bensmathreps!

2. Make a bunch of copies, since you are going to use different numbers with the same math mat over a period of days. Typically, I make enough for five reps for the whole class. You can also stick these into sheet protectors if you want to save paper.

Instructions

1. Display the paper version of the MathReps. Work through the paper version together. The first few times, we will do the reps together. I like to give students a copy of the paper and follow along as we fill out each section. As students progress, we review the MathReps together, and I focus on any parts the students are struggling with. Different stu-

dents can also come up and help fill out the different sections of the MathRep. Most of the time, students are on the carpet using clipboards with a pencil or markers.

2. When students are confident enough to try the MathRep on their own, they can be released to their seats. Usually, I will scaffold this release. In the beginning, I will leave the collectively completed MathRep on the document camera so students can refer to it if they need to. As students gain mastery, I will cover up certain portions of the MathRep with sticky notes. Before I think students are ready, I will remove the whole paper and have students try it on their own. This gives me an idea of which students are struggling with different skills, and I can then pull a small group the next time we do MathReps with them. I like to give students a time limit of about seven to ten minutes once they are familiar with the reps. As an early finisher activity, students can get their Play-Doh out and represent the number they are working on in different ways.

3. After time is up, we review the MathReps under the document camera. Students come back to the carpet, and we check over the reps to see how we did. I cover up the names as we look at them and ask students to reflect on some of the reps. You can ask questions like, "What did the student do well?" or "Do you see anything that needs to be improved?" Students can share their responses with their partners before we discuss them as a class. We try to keep the pace snappy as we review to keep students engaged in their learning.

Ben
Even though we start these on paper, we transition to doing the same skill in Seesaw very quickly. Because they mirror each other, students catch on really quickly, plus they get to record their thinking in Seesaw.

Ben
I start MathReps at the beginning of the year with my mini MathReps number booklet, which is a super simplified version. We start with the number 1 and do a number every day until we reach 10!

Ben
Why markers? Markers or colors make it more fun. Plus, I can use two markers to represent two different groups to make one number. Just remember the number used for one color should be consistent across the MathRep.

Jenn's Way (1st-2nd)

I have taught TK, first, and second grade. As a result, I really understand how mathematical concepts and standards not only work together but also progress year to year. One thing I've noticed as I taught different grade levels was that students acted surprised each time I taught the next part of a concept. It was as though they were never taught the skill before, even though I knew they had been because I had taught those grade levels. Then I came across Lisa Nowakowski's MathReps. I was immediately intrigued and needed to find out more about how this concept worked. I started to integrate Lisa's templates, and I saw a HUGE change in my students' understanding of the concepts—which meant that MathReps worked, and I needed more.

I understand that students need repetition, practice, and to constantly be exposed to material in order for it to sink in. I personally feel this is especially important in the TK–2 classrooms because we are building the foundation for student success. I took Lisa's model, and I went with it.

One of the biggest changes I made when adapting MathReps for TK–2 was putting it into Seesaw. Besides that, my version of MathReps is very similar; I just change the standards being covered to match our pacing guide.

Basically, similar to Little p*ARTS, I start with certain mathematical concepts, usually the main standards we cover in first grade, including some that are taught right away and some that are taught later. This way, when we get to the concepts being taught later, students have a lot of prior knowledge and experience. This means that teaching that concept takes less time because students already have an understanding of it from constantly reviewing it.

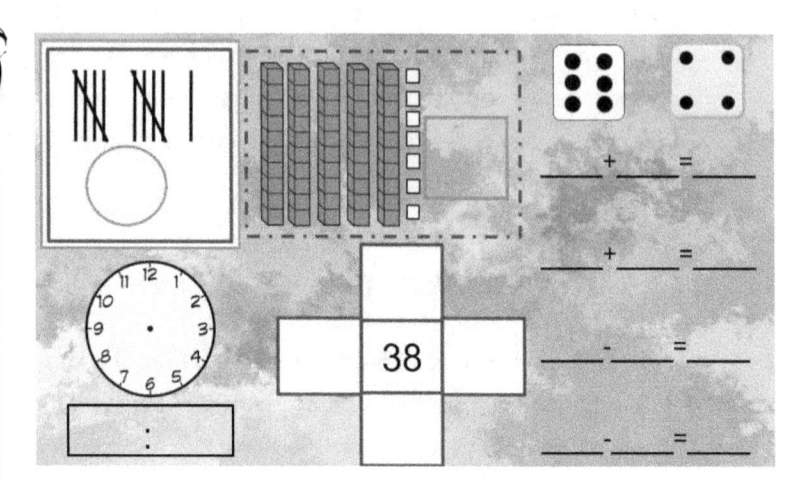

TK–2 MathReps templates from MathReps.com

Jenn

In this example, I added in the clock because telling time is one of the last mathematical standards we teach, yet it is heavily related to number sense and often confuses students. By front-loading and teaching how the numbers on the clock work with number sense, students are better able to master the concept and see how these concepts work together.

A MathRep with the clock embedded alongside number sense skills.

Once you make or select a template for MathReps, the next step is to actually teach the rep. I am not going to lie, this takes time. In fact, this is often my math lesson for the day: I literally teach each concept for the template. We do this together in an interactive lesson. Students have their own copy of the template, and I teach how to count the tallies, then the place value blocks, etc.

We do this concept review every single day with less and less modeling as students begin to understand the EduProtocol and the concepts being taught. Then this review starts to become partner practice. I am also able to use this as individual assessment for data when I need to, because now the students understand the protocol. I am not assessing their test-taking skills, but instead I am assessing their mastery of concepts and standards.

As students continue to grow and learn, I begin to change some of the concepts. In this example, we took away tally marks and added in word problems with three addends.

As students gain familiarity with MathReps, we keep the other standards but alter them slightly. One concept that is extremely difficult for many students is 10 more and 10 less starting at any number. In order for the class to master it, we keep it on our MathReps all year (or close to it) but change where we add 10 more and 10 less. As I change the standards covered, it is still constantly being reviewed. I am doing less teaching and more independent/partner practice. In fact, this becomes a center. After we do our math lesson for the day, students have this as their partner activity and once a week as their individual assessment. I use it for data collection to know what standards need more practice, which students need additional help, and which standards I can move on from for a while before I integrate them again later.

> **Ben**
>
> Just like Jenn says, the first time you teach a MathRep, it might be your whole lesson. I also love how she mentions data! After students complete a MathRep, I like to make two piles, one pile for students that got it, and one pile for students who may need some intervention.

> **Jenn**
>
> I tend to wait to add the word problems because students struggle with the reading portion in the beginning of the year. Once we get some great reading foundations and start teaching how to read math word problems like a story, I start to add them more and more.

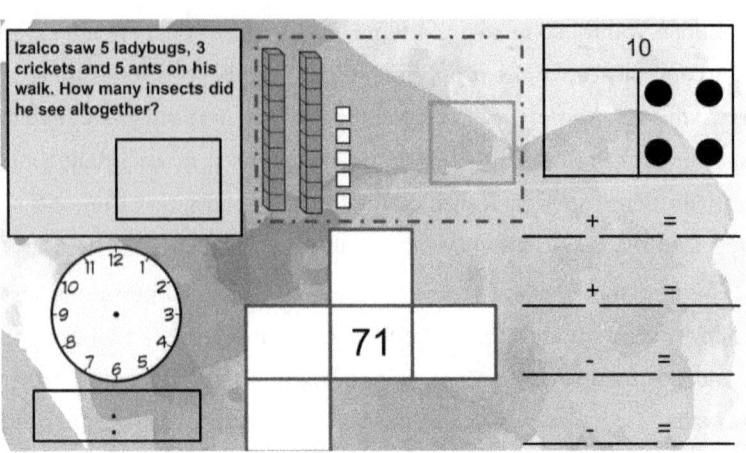

A MathRep in which the 10 less box has moved

Preparation

1. Make or select your MathReps template (see Extended Content)
   - First-Grade Google Slides MathReps
   - Second-Grade Google Slides MathReps
   - First-Grade Printable Version of MathReps
   - Second-Grade Printable Version of MathReps
2. Assign it to your students or print it off to pass out to students.

Instruction

1. Have students open the assignment with you, whether you assigned it digitally or printed it on paper.
2. Teach the first part of the MathRep. Have students complete it with you.
3. Repeat for each standard/concept. Spend as much time as needed on each section. Some parts will be easier than others. This is your teaching time.
4. Review concepts over and over again, until students are really ready to try the MathRep with a partner. I usually do this for at least a week. Then we transition to partners, and I walk around the room, teaching in the moment. Eventually

---

Ben

Working or walking around the room is so important. It is a great opportunity to give students immediate feedback.

that MathRep can become a center in which students either work with partners or independently.

5. Change the standards and mix up the MathRep. Be sure to change only one or two at a time because the point is to constantly review standards and concepts.

6. Repeat MathReps at least 2-3 days a week.

Extended Content:
MathReps

MathReps is great on paper, but can also be very powerful when we blend it with technology. MathReps can also be paired with Fast & Curious.

In the extended content, you'll get:
- ★ Some benefits to using digital tools for MathReps
- ★ Ideas for building even more mathematical vocabulary
- ★ Tips on how to make MathReps even more accessible for students
- ★ Templates, resources, student examples, and more

My notes:

How It Looks in Seesaw	Templates & Resources	Student Examples
tinyurl.com/MathRepsSeesaw Password: 73468	tinyurl.com/MathRepsFolder	tinyurl.com/MathRepsExamples

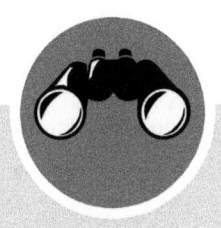

Chapter 12
Sketch and Tell EduProtocol

"All right, students, what was the main idea of that story? Let's get out our paper and write." As the teacher walks around the classroom, some students begin writing right away, while other students just sit there struggling with even the simplest idea. Does this sound familiar?

It should, because for many teachers, getting primary kids to form an idea and write in one step is a challenge. But if we can visualize our response and draw it first, we might have a head start. In fact, many primary journals or primary writing paper templates have space at the top for a drawing, so with the Sketch and Tell EduProtocol we leverage that space to our students' advantage!

Sketch and Tell should be a simple transition for many primary teachers. However, it is not always traditional for the kids. Not all kids come to school knowing how to sketch anything, let alone have the background knowledge about the topic they are about to learn about. The good news is that it can be something that all students can do easily to share their learning. How? By implementing the EduProtocol Sketch and Tell!

Academic Goals

- Help students explain their thinking about any concept
- Students learn collaboration skills
- Students develop and expand their writing skills
- Students gain the opportunity to share their thinking in multiple ways

Teacher Big Ideas

- Build students' language skills before running the Sketch and Tell EduProtocol.

- Give students the opportunity to listen and share ideas.
- Give students a chance to share in-person and then record their thinking to provide more reps.
- This can be adapted in numerous ways.

Original EduProtocol: Sketch and Tell

In the original Sketch and Tell EduProtocol, students read a text or watch a video clip. Typically, there is a guiding question or prompt students will address in a sketch response. Sometimes this can be wholly open-ended (draw your favorite food, etc.).

Students may watch a video about the water cycle and how water circulates in the environment. The guiding question/prompt might be "What happens to the water after it rains?" Students then sketch their response to the question. After sketching, students participate in the "Tell" part, which involves two parts: a structured think-pair-share (structured because they are using their picture to support the retelling/explanation) and then a short written explanation about their sketch. When Marlena Hebern created Sketch and Tell, she wanted to make sure that English language learners had an opportunity to orally share their understanding of something they heard, read, or saw before writing. The pair share in Sketch and Tell is an oral practice before the writing, which is beneficial not only for our English language students but for all students. Students also take turns listening to their partner(s) explain the concept of their sketch.

Sketch and Tell Steps

1. Provide students with a resource such as a textbook selection, article, or video.
2. Prep: Ask the students your posing question. It could be as simple as "What is the main idea of this passage?" or more specific, such as "What are the layers of the earth or parts of a plant?"
3. Read: Students will read or watch the resource.

4. Sketch: Students sketch out their learning/make a schematic or diagram. Note: this is not art; this is modeling and nonlinguistic communication. Art skills are not required—we love stick people. Students are amazingly creative when using the Shapes tool in Seesaw, Google Slides, or PowerPoint as well. No drawing skills needed, just creativity.

5. Share: Students will tell a partner about their visual. Have them make sure to tell at least 2–4 details about their sketch.

6. Tell: After sharing, students write can make a three-item list or an explanatory paragraph answering the question posed by the teacher.

Ben & Jenn

Amanda Sandoval is a phenomenal educator who created this exquisite template to help you get started with Sketch and Tell: tinyurl.com/sandovalSAT.

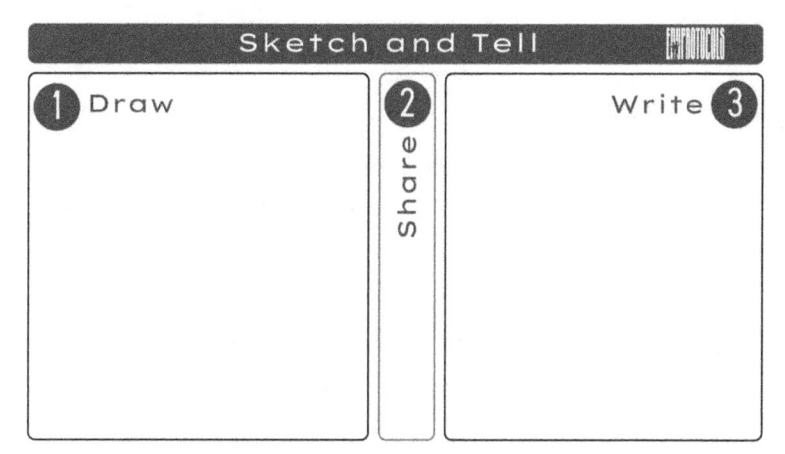

Sketch and Tell

① Draw ② Share Write ③

Sketch and Tell Template

Our Way (Kindergarten–2nd)

If you have noticed the pattern to this book, first Ben gives his kindergarten take, and then Jenn gives her take. However, we both run this EduProtocol in a similar way. And we both have some remix options that we will address below.

We both love to run this protocol on paper as well as in Seesaw. Note that one major difference in our variation from the original EduProtocol is that we do not always have students write a sentence. Instead, we just make sure to hit the key points, which are to sketch a drawing and tell about it in some way.

> **Ben & Jenn**
>
> We say step 1 is optional because you don't really have to prepare anything ahead of time. You can pick a text or concept, pick a question or prompt, and then just go. Did someone say low prep?

Preparation

1. Prepare a template for the activity to share with students. This can be as simple as a piece of paper that students draw a line down the middle of and write *sketch* on one side and *tell* on the other, or as elaborate as you want it to be. You can assign a Seesaw activity with nothing attached or simply have students add their own page.
2. Decide on the essential standard, concept, or driving question you want your students to focus on.
3. Pick a nonfiction text, read-aloud story, video, concept, or mini-lesson to use for the activity.

Instructions

1. Introduce a topic, media, or prompt to students. Show students the media clip or images, or read the text or book.
2. Have students engage in discussion around the topic, images, media, or prompt.
3. On paper or digitally, have students draw their ideas as related to the topic prompt or media.
4. Have students share their drawings with other students.
5. Have students write words or sentences related to their ideas and/or record their thinking.

> **Ben & Jenn**
>
> Of course, we love using Seesaw for Sketch and Tell because of the ease of use and access to the drawing tools.

Ben's Way (Kindergarten)

Our adapted Sketch and Tell EduProtocol is fairly similar to the original protocol, but we have expanded opportunities for language as well as different ways for students to sketch or represent their knowledge. Plus, we don't always take it to writing, but instead we do a lot of telling via recording.

For starters, I try to build as much language as possible for my kindergartners. In a typical activity, teachers might present some knowledge, have the kids think-pair-share, and then start said activity. However, I find this structure does not give my littles, especially

> **Marlena**
>
> Recording is an excellent way for young students to express their learning, especially pre-readers and writers.

my English language learners, enough opportunities to practice language.

Since "Tell" is a key part of this EduProtocol, I try to add a few more opportunities within the lesson. I rely on my English speakers or students with more background knowledge and vocabulary to help provide models for students who need them.

Here are a few ways to build in more vocabulary and language before students actually Sketch and Tell on their own.

- Practice a Sketch and Tell together, model the think-pair-share with students, and then allow some students to model recording their thinking. Then, listen to the recordings after. This is helpful in the beginning when some students may not know what to say about their sketches.
- Ask students what they know about a topic before you begin. Displaying an image or picture can help a lot.
- Read or watch the media multiple times, stopping to highlight key words or sections, and perhaps even taking a few notes on the board. Sometimes, I like to read a book and then watch the book as a read-aloud on YouTube. That way, students get a few different views of the same text. (Story comprehension is a great place to start with Sketch and Tell.)
- Before students think-pair-share, give students an opportunity to share out loud what they may know to model responses for less verbal students.
- Give students a chance to share with multiple partners. On the carpet, students have front, back, and side-to-side partners. Getting students up and moving with a partner picker or tool can also help keep students engaged and sharing. Flippity.net is a great free tool with which you can make pairs or any size group.
- Provide anchor charts with visuals and/or key vocabulary for easy reference.
- There are many other ways to engage students in language, but giving students multiple opportunities to share and listen will set up students for success. Even with multiple op-

Jenn
Did you read that? Our TK-2 students need practice with language. They need to practice how to use language to talk and tell about things.

Ben
I like to have some students share with the whole class before I have them turn to a partner. I find this helps some of my language learners frame what they might want to say, and they are more successful when they talk to a partner.

Jenn
Another strategy I use is a talking frame. This is not something they need forever, but it can help them to build those language foundations and gain confidence in sharing.

Jenn
I like to set a timer and tell students to see how many partners they can share with before the timer goes off. (Reps!) I also like to ask them what their partner said when we return to the carpet to help encourage students to listen and learn from each other.

Ben & Jenn

We love getting students to talk, and we really appreciate some of the Spencer Kagan strategies. These structures give students many different ways to engage in partnerships and make sure everyone is learning.

Ben

By *tell*, I mean two things: Have students share with at least one person. Have them record it in Seesaw. Combine these two tasks, and this is a great way to tell.

Ben

This is a great protocol to have students practice for opinion writing and goes well with Would You Rather, as mentioned in the Smart Start section. I love to use this protocol to share what their favorite _____ is! When students share their favorites, it is a great way to build language and vocabulary, and to practice stating and defending an opinion.

portunities, I make sure to personally check in with students who may need some extra help.

- There are so many ways students can Sketch and Tell! I particularly love using Seesaw because I can have students draw something and then easily record themselves telling all about it. Here are some of my favorite ways to Sketch and Tell:

  - Sketch yourself making a good choice in the classroom, and tell me why it is a good choice.
  - Sketch how you are feeling about _____, and tell me why you are feeling that way.
  - Sketch your favorite part of the book, and tell me what your favorite part was and why.
  - Sketch your favorite _____ (anything), and tell me why it is your favorite.

After we went on a field trip to the aquarium, students came back and **sketched** what they saw. Then they recorded themselves **telling** all about it. They next day we wrote about the trip, and it was much easier for students since they had already brainstormed with Sketch and Tell.

A Sketch and Tell EduProtocol about the aquarium

In this super fun example, we read Dragons Love Tacos. We then **sketched** our favorite taco. Then **told** about what toppings we liked on our tacos. This was a fun class building activity, and was a great connection to the books as well.

A Sketch and Tell EduProtocol about *Dragons Love Tacos*

- Sketch a word that begins with _____ , and tell me about the word (segment and blend and use it in a sentence).
- Sketch a connection you had to the text, and tell me about how the connection relates to you.
- Sketch what you think will happen next in the text, and tell me how you came up with that conclusion.
- Sketch the number _____, and tell me about how you represented the number.
- Sketch the shape _____, and tell me the key attributes of that shape.
- Sketch the weather _____, and tell me about this type of weather.

If you don't already have a ton of ideas, you are in for a treat. Jenn and I have found many ways for students to "sketch" their knowledge. For example, students can build or create something out of Lego, blocks/Unifix cubes, Play-Doh, or virtually any other manipulatives, and then tell about their creation. You can check this out after Jenn's awesome section.

Jenn's Way (1st-2nd)

Sketch and Tell is one of my favorite EduProtocols to start with because sketching is already something many students are familiar with, especially after we do Smart Start. The simple act of sketching covers not only multiple standards but also fine motor skills, and telling builds oral language as well as collaboration skills. So how do we do Sketch and Tell in first and second grade?

Basically, we take what Ben does in the kindergarten version and take it to the next level by giving students lots of background knowledge, vocabulary, and chances to collaborate and share. The difference between kindergarten and first and second grade is the time it takes to get to a more independent level and the way in which we "tell."

The first thing I do when leading Sketch and Tell is introduce the topic. Let's say we are going to be learning about making the num-

Marlena

It's okay that these modifications deviate from the original Sketch and Tell. Just keep in mind that the original Sketch and Tell was all about assisting students in processing what they hear, see, and watch and developing oral language to support their comprehension.

> **Jenn**
> This can also be done using technology. In that case, students would pull out their device and open the assignment.

ber ten. We would start by introducing the number 10 and then practice making the number 10 together. This is something students learn in kindergarten, too, but we really solidify it in first grade as we focus on number sense and how groups of ten work in our entire system. After doing a mini-lesson on how to decompose the number ten, students pull out their Sketch and Tell paper.

On the sketch side, students show one way to make the number 10. In the example, students use Seesaw to draw a way to make the number 10 on a ten frame. However, Sketch and Tell can be more open-ended than that. In this example, students record themselves telling a story to match their ten-frame sketch. They actually move the unicorns and dragons to tell a story that makes the number 10. For example, 4 unicorns were flying in the sky trying to find a rainbow. Instead, they found a huge cave. They went inside and 6 dragons were practicing breathing fire. The unicorns thought that would be fun. Now there are 10 magical creatures in the cave together because 4 + 6 = 10.

However, if the Seesaw element seems like too much, you don't have to tell it that way. Other ways for students to tell might include:

1. Simply showing their drawing to a partner and telling them how they made the number 10.
2. Writing the addition sentence that matches the sketch.
3. Adding a video orally telling how they made the number 10.
4. Building a matching model with Unifix cubes and showing the parts in a video.

In the first- and second-grade classroom, we like to share things as a group instead of only with partners. This allows for more collaboration and helps students continue to build their language and learn from each other. In this example, the students are in groups of four and shared with each other.

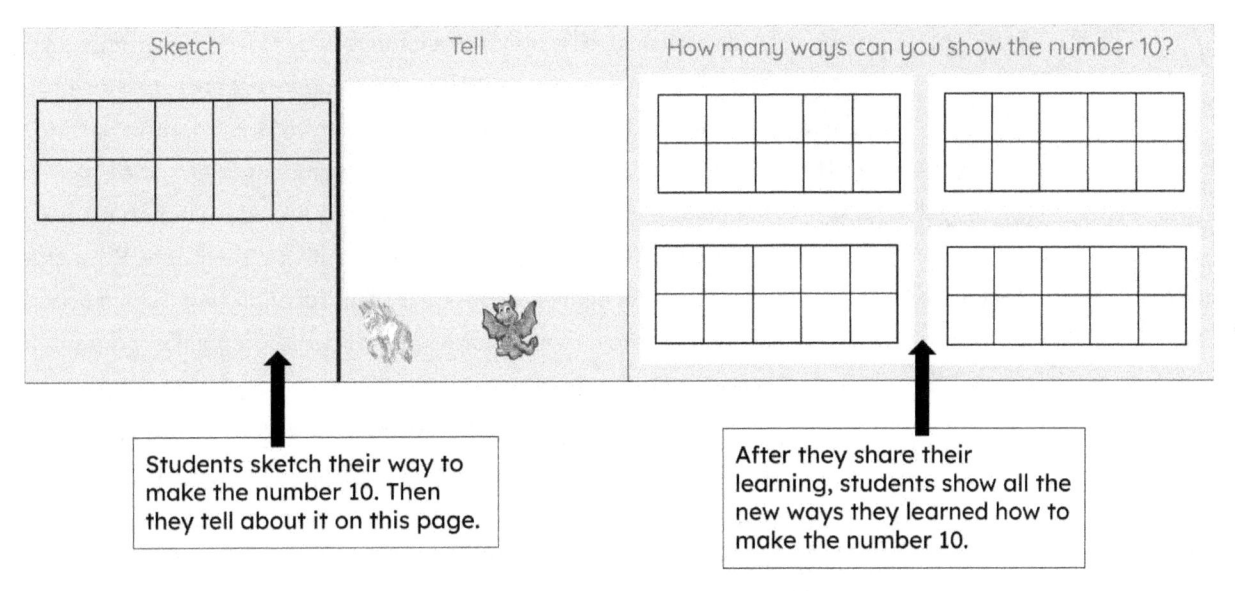

Chapter 12 | Sketch and Tell EduProtocol | 121

| Sketch | Tell | How many ways can you show the number 10? |

Students sketch their way to make the number 10. Then they tell about it on this page.

After they share their learning, students show all the new ways they learned how to make the number 10.

A structured math Sketch and Tell

After they share, then they show what they learned by adding to their sketch on another page. Now instead of one way to make the number 10, students have learned at least four different ways to make the number 10. The best part about this EduProtocol is that it can be done with just about anything. Making a 10 is just one simple example, but the possibilities go much further.

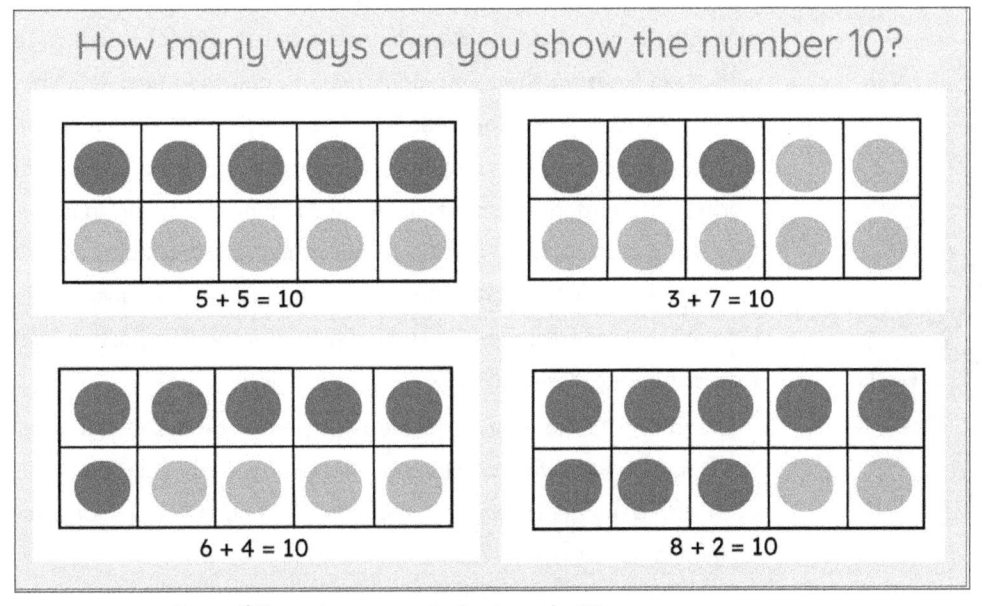

How many ways can you show the number 10?

5 + 5 = 10

3 + 7 = 10

6 + 4 = 10

8 + 2 = 10

Four different ways a student made 10

> **Jenn**
>
> I still let students record when they move on to writing the tell side. They either record reading their writing or add a video to summarize what they wrote. Now we're practicing skills like summarizing. So many standards and skills learned in one protocol!

> **Jenn**
>
> Fun alert! Have them sketch a vacation destination billboard and then use a video for the "tell" part to create a commercial convincing others to choose their vacation spot. Students write the script for their commercial.

A student explains their Build and Tell with Seesaw.

tinyurl.com/seesawstudentvoice

Sketch and Tell is also a phenomenal way to work on writing skills. Focusing on narrative writing? Have students sketch their favorite memory and share about it. Working toward informative writing? Have students watch a video on the animal of their choice, sketch the animal, and write a paragraph on the tell side. What about opinion writing? As a class, research different vacation spots. Have students form an opinion about their ideal vacation spot, sketch it, and encourage their own research skills to write an opinion paragraph with supporting details.

The key to using this EduProtocol in the TK-2 classroom is scaffolding it. The more you use it, the more familiar students get with it, and the more independence they develop. In fact, this becomes one of my favorite independent center lessons that students can complete as I am working with small groups. Start simple, work your way up, and be amazed at what these kids can do and teach each other.

Remix Time

Build and Tell

Build and Tell is a fun way for students to practice language and creativity (plus other Four Cs). You can do this variation on Sketch and Tell a bunch of different ways, from a Design Thinking Challenge with Lego to using shape manipulatives to create letters. Students can do these activities on Seesaw using the picture feature or the drag and drop. Students can label the picture to practice individual words, write sentences, or even just record themselves sharing about their picture. In fact, just having students just take a picture, record, and share about their creation is a great way to build descriptive language. Of course, make sure students share with a partner and their computer for extra reps.

Build and Tell can be performed with many different materials. You can do it with wooden blocks, linking cubes, Play-Doh, clay, and even with a puzzle. It can be a group build, a partner build, or even an individual activity.

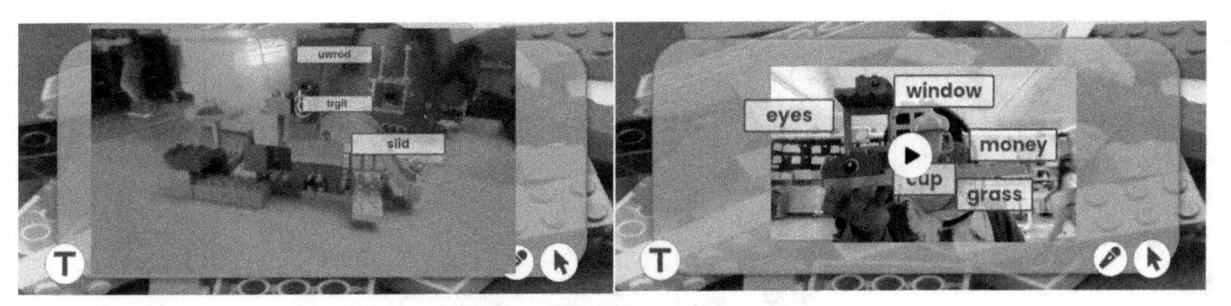

Build and Tell with Lego in Seesaw

Students really enjoy building items they were studying, like ladybugs and butterflies. In our classes, we start with building simple items that students are familiar with, like cats and dogs, and then we move on to more complicated builds, like parks and houses. Adding some creative constraints, like limiting the number of pieces or setting a time limit, can spice up the challenge even more.

Ben
Students love this activity because they get to be creative, plus as a bonus they practice typing words. I love hearing them use their sounds as they label the different parts of their creations.

Jenn
Notice anything? It can be done using anything and in any way! So many possibilities. How are your students going to Build and Tell tomorrow?

Build and Tell with Lego on Paper

Ben

Remember that after students build, they can share with a partner or partners, and then tell by creating a video in Seesaw.

Student creates a number problem using Unifix cubes and records their thinking in Seesaw.

Another effective way to Build and Tell is to use Unifix cubes. Students can use one color to build a number or, better yet, two colors to build a number. For example, the number 5 can be made up of four yellow cubes and one blue cube. Students create some great mathematical language when they describe different ways to make a number. It also helps them build conceptual understanding. This activity leads nicely into addition and number sentences. You can give students a number to create or have them choose their own number. You can also have students create the same number in as many different ways as possible.

One more awesome Build and Tell activity is with 2-D and 3-D shapes. All you really need are some marshmallows and toothpicks with which students can build each shape. Then students can record themselves telling all about the attributes of the shape, such as the number of vertices/corners and sides. As a bonus, you can even have the student sketch the shapes. You can do this with 2-D shapes or 3-D shapes. You can also have students compare different shapes.

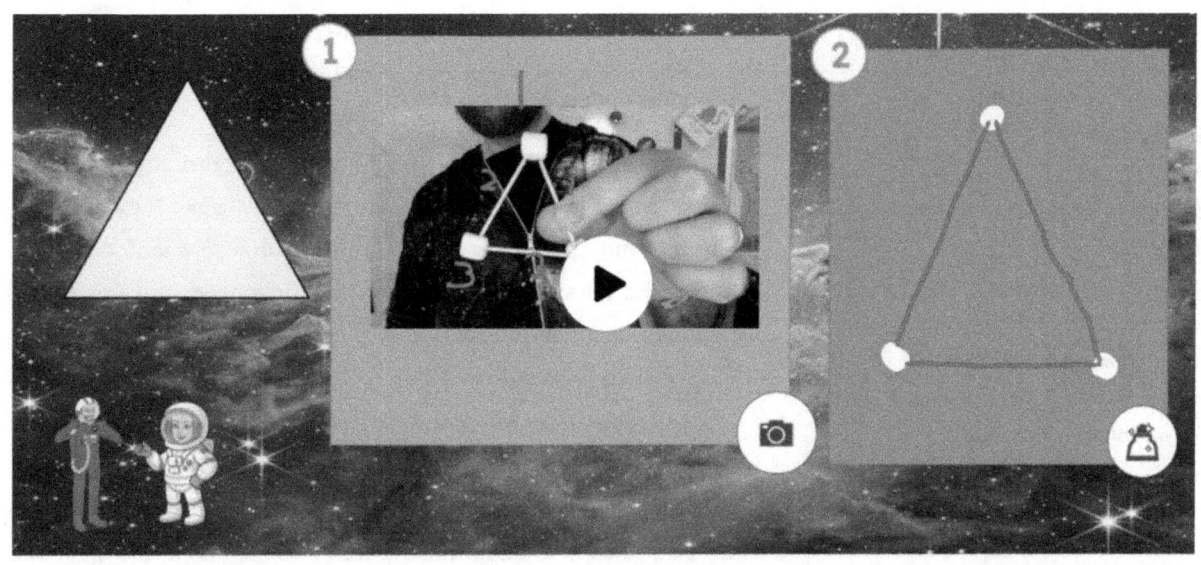

Students build 2-D shapes using marshmallows and toothpicks and tell/record their explanation in Seesaw.

Code and Tell

We know how important computer science is in today's world, but it can be difficult to integrate it into the TK–2 classroom when we have so many other things that we are responsible for. Instead of making computer science "one more thing to do," it can become a part of the other things we are doing. Code and Tell is an adaptation of Sketch and Tell that helps combine computer science with many other standards.

For example, one of our favorite ways to use Sketch and Tell is to retell stories. We can make retelling stories more engaging and also teach coding skills at the same time! But how? The first step is to read a story to the students or have students read the story on their own. After students have heard or read the story, it is time to retell it, but instead of sketching the beginning, middle, and end, they are going to work on coding it.

Have students open their coding program. One we suggest that is very TK–2 friendly is ScratchJr. Students can start to look at the characters, settings, and actions in order to think about how they want to retell their story. Then, after having some time to explore, students can start to sketch their code. They can sketch what setting they are

> **Ben**
>
> Some of my favorite tools for coding can be found on the Hour of Code website. I love the Foos and Kodable, which have free tutorials via the Hour or Code. Students can run the code and then tell all about how they programmed it. It is so simple and fun that even kindergartners can do it.

> **Ben & Jenn**
>
> There are lots of great codable robots that kindergarten students can use. Bee-Bot by Terrapin is one of our favorites because all of the buttons are right on top of the robot. There are a few other robots like Bee-Bot. For us, the key is to find ones that have the buttons for coding right on top. That makes it simpler for students and requires no extra technology.

going to use, which characters they are going to use, and even what they want the characters to say. Sketching is how students first plan and organize their thoughts for retelling the story.

Once their sketch is done, they can use the program to create their code. This is where students start the "tell" part. They program their code and run it when it is done. They can record their code and put it on the Tell side. This is a little more advanced, and something we suggest for first and second grade, but there are so many ways to do this with TK-K students, too!

In one of the examples above, students are shown a way to make the number 10. They have to draw and then record themselves telling how they made the number 10. However, you can also do this with coding "a robot"! You can make a mat like the one in the example. Students look at it and decide how they are going to make the number 10. They have to think about the directions their robot will take. Do they need to go forward, backward, left, or right?

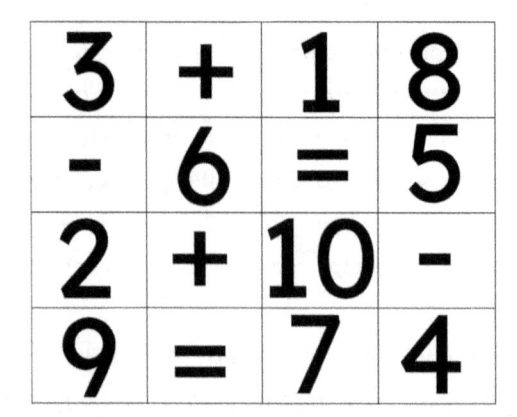

3	+	1	8
-	6	=	5
2	+	10	-
9	=	7	4

A number mat used in conjunction with a robot

As students are looking at the mat, they can use the template to sketch the directions the robot will take to make the number ten. This is done by simply drawing the arrows. Notice they have to use the +, -, and = signs to tell their way to make the number 10. After they sketch their code, they can practice running the code. If it does not work, they can fix their sketch and try again. Once they have their code programmed correctly, they record their code. Now they've just practiced critical thinking skills to code their way of making the number 10, integrated computer science, and mastered an essential mathematical standard.

A Seesaw template for Code and Tell

Sketch
(boxes 1–8)

Students sketch their code on the sketch side.

Tell

Students record their robot doing the code on the tell side.

Jenn

Once you have a template for a robot mat, you can change what's in the boxes. For example, you can insert letters, CVC words, or sight words. Students can have fun coding and playing. Lots of possibilities!

There are so many other ways to Code and Tell:

- Code a robot to make a specific shape.
- Code a robot like Dash to play a song you are learning.
- Code a robot to show a sound and light pattern, focusing on ways the sounds and lights change.
- Code the robot to find certain sight words and record playing the game.

she	have	see	there
in	was	on	like
were	the	here	now
of	no	he	saw

Another example of a robot mat with sight words

Extended Content:
Sketch and Tell

Sketch and Tell is one of the best EduProtocols for building oral language. We can maximize this even more when we add student recording to this protocol.

In the extended content, you'll get:
★ Benefits of using a digital tool for Sketch and Tell
★ Several ideas and examples on how to use Seesaw to maximize Sketch and Tell
★ Templates, resources, student examples, and more

Notes:

How It Looks in Seesaw	Templates & Resources	Student Examples
tinyurl.com/SKATseesaw Password: 73468	tinyurl.com/sketchandtellfolder	tinyurl.com/SketchTellExamples

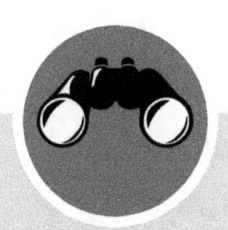

Chapter 13
Racking and Stacking EduProtocols

Stacking EduProtocols refers to arranging several reps of the same EduProtocol in a single lesson or unit. Racking and Stacking EduProtocols refers to combining two or more different EduProtocols into one lesson or unit.

What's better than one EduProtocol? Racking and Stacking several EduProtocols! Once you are feeling confident with your integration of EduProtocols, the next step is to start combining them. How can they work together to make learning more engaging? How can you save yourself time and give students immediate feedback that helps them be successful? Racking and Stacking EduProtocols does just that! Here are some of our favorite ways to Rack and Stack EduProtocols in the K–2 classroom.

Ben & Jenn
We wanted to make sure to put in a quick review of each protocol we are racking and stacking. Hopefully these refreshers will help you own and internalize the EduProtocols even more.

Racking and Stacking Fast and Curious

As mentioned in previous chapters, Fast and Curious (FAC) involves using a digital assessment tool to quickly assess what students know. You then write the class percentage somewhere where students can see how they did. You look at the data to reteach the key points the class needs to review, spending more time on the questions the majority of students struggled with. After doing a quick reteach, you run the digital assessment tool/game again. Write the new class percentage to show how much they grew in a quick protocol. Although this protocol is phenomenal on its own, it is even better when Racked and Stacked with other EduProtocols. How? Let's see!

Fast and Curious + MathReps

MathReps are essential to ensuring that all students can truly master math standards and love and understand math. However, let's be real: keeping kids engaged in learning throughout the day can be difficult. How you teach math can also depend on how much energy or attention the students have in order to really learn the content. That is why racking and stacking MathReps with Fast and Curious can be so effective. The gamified concept of FAC gets the students engaged in what they are learning. Additionally, they get the immediate feedback they need. Students can see which questions they need help with, get retaught in the moment, and then redeem themselves with the MathReps activity. Just remember, primary students have tiny attention spans, so this Rack and Stack may be done over more than one session.

Racking and stacking these EduProtocols can be done in so many ways. One of our favorite ways to do this is to launch an FAC that matches the MathReps activity.

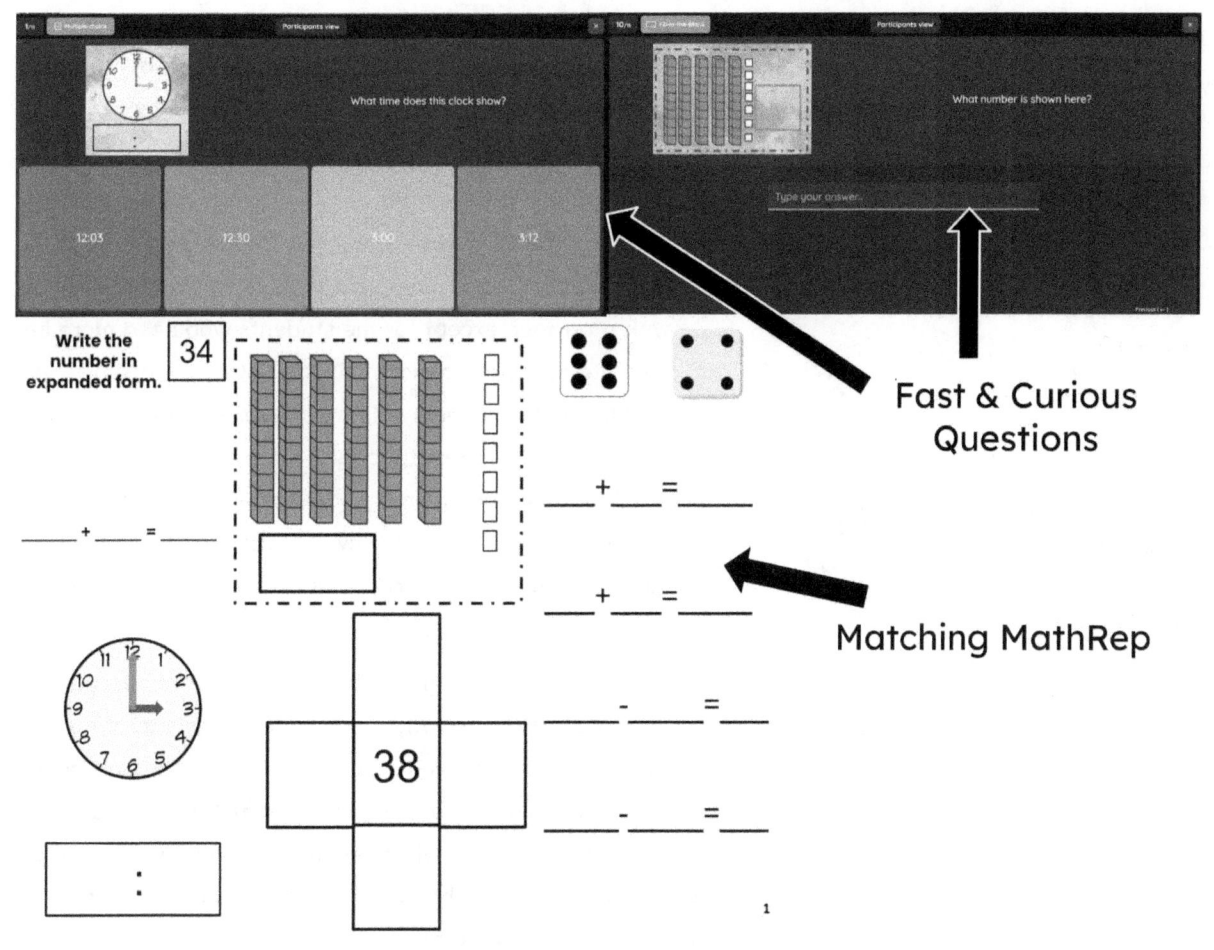

Chapter 13 | Racking and Stacking EduProtocols | 131

A Fast and Curious Rack and Stack supports a MathRep.

1. Using any tool that you prefer, find or create a quiz with the same exact questions that are on your MathReps for the day. In the example, you can see we are telling time to the hour, writing the expanded form, counting tens and ones, etc. The questions on the FAC are the exact same questions as this MathRep.

2. First, we run the FAC EduProtocol as usual. We write the class percentage on the board under the words *Round 1*.

3. Then we pass out the MathReps paper. We use this as our reteach/immediate feedback time. We use the data from the FAC to tell us which parts of the MathRep we need to focus on the most.

> **Jenn**
>
> What I love about this is that you don't have to wait for data. The data is in real time, and I can help teach students right then, in the moment, helping to ensure concrete understanding of mathematical standards.

> **Ben**
>
> We love to blend these digital and analog tools. You can always do a MathRep on paper, followed up by a Fast and Curious online. This is a great way to support student instruction.

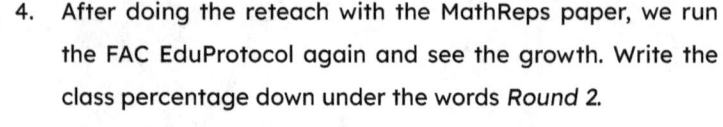

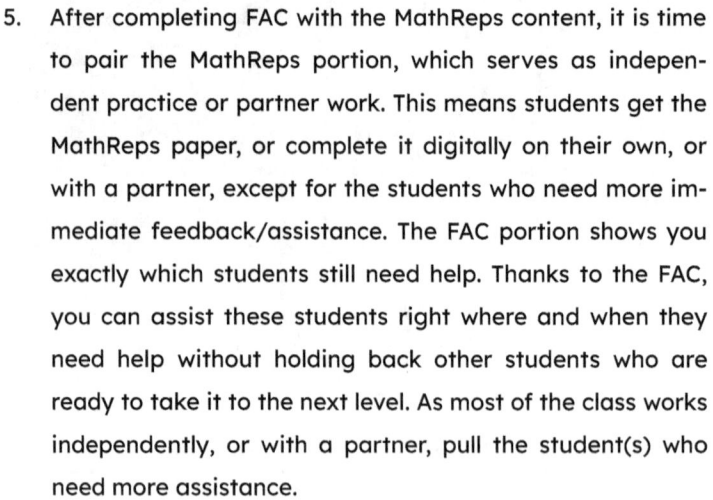

4. After doing the reteach with the MathReps paper, we run the FAC EduProtocol again and see the growth. Write the class percentage down under the words *Round 2*.

5. After completing FAC with the MathReps content, it is time to pair the MathReps portion, which serves as independent practice or partner work. This means students get the MathReps paper, or complete it digitally on their own, or with a partner, except for the students who need more immediate feedback/assistance. The FAC portion shows you exactly which students still need help. Thanks to the FAC, you can assist these students right where and when they need help without holding back other students who are ready to take it to the next level. As most of the class works independently, or with a partner, pull the student(s) who need more assistance.

As you get used to racking and stacking EduProtocols, you will discover that there are other ways you can do it! Instead of running the typical FAC live model, you can assign the digital assessment tool to be completed in an asynchronous format. Students can complete the FAC portion completely independently. Remember, though, when assigning in an asynchronous format, it is beneficial to use a tool that allows students to play as many times as they want and review their answers. This way, they get that same immediate feedback and can continue to practice until mastery.

With this variation, once students go through their self-paced FAC, they complete the MathReps by themselves (or with a partner). What do you think happens as you continue to do this? Do you see how the students are becoming more and more independent? This EduProtocol rack and stack starts with you helping them to see their immediate feedback and teaching according to that feedback, but it ends with students learning how to get their feedback by themselves. Ultimately, this rack and stack leads to more time, less grading, and students who do not just achieve good test scores but truly master concepts, standards, and so much more!

Fast and Curious + Sketch and Tell

We LOVE racking and stacking these two EduProtocols because, again, the possibilities are endless. Literally anything you are learning about can be thrown in Fast and Curious. Learning about light and sound waves in your science unit? Run FAC on it. Learning about US landmarks or states and capitals in your social studies unit? Run FAC on it. Learning how to retell stories in the correct sequence in ELA? Run FAC on a story you just read. Learning how to make numbers using place value blocks in math? Run FAC on it. Do you see how this can literally be done with any content/standard? Use the data to do some reteaching, and run the EduProtocol again to help students show what they learned.

Then, to get students to take it to the next level, have them Sketch and Tell about the lesson! Students do a quick sketch to show what they learned. Then they tell their partner about it. Maybe they sketch a number with place value blocks and then tell about how many hundreds, tens, and ones they used and what number it makes. Maybe they sketch their story sequence and retell what happened in the story. Or maybe they sketch a state and draw where the capital is located and then tell about it. The best part of this protocol is it allows for so much student choice. Students could sketch on paper or do it digitally. Let them choose.

After they sketch, they get more choices for the tell part. Do they want to tell about what they learned by writing out a few sentences or a paragraph (depending on grade level)? Do they want to take a picture using a digital tool (like Seesaw) and add voice, video, or a label to type? They have several options in how they tell what they learn. Of course, after they Sketch and Tell, you have the option to run another FAC to close the lesson out. By racking and stacking these two EduProtocols, students are more engaged in the learning process, have more time to practice with the information they are learning, and are then more successful in showing what they learned.

Jenn

Giving students choices promotes student agency. By simply allowing students to choose their tool or how they share their learning, you have more buy in, make the learning more accessible and relevant, and help students to become independent learners and thinkers.

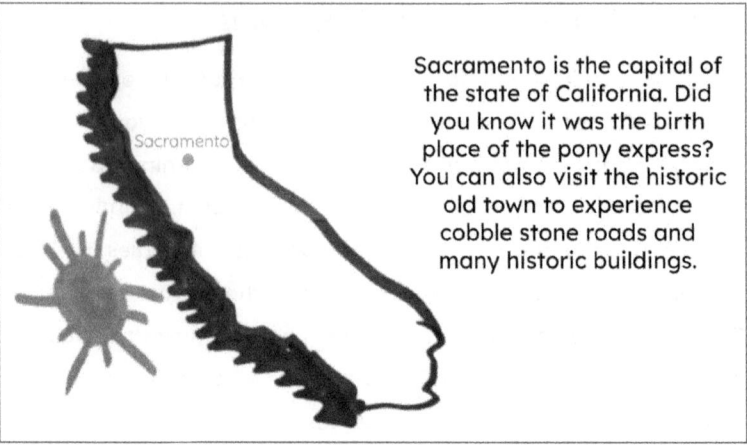

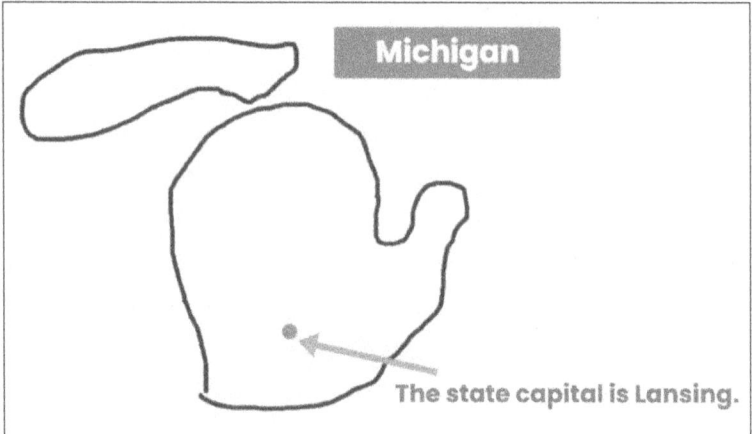

Sacramento is the capital of the state of California. Did you know it was the birth place of the pony express? You can also visit the historic old town to experience cobble stone roads and many historic buildings.

Michigan

The state capital is Lansing.

Student Sketch and Tell work samples

Ben's Morning Message

The morning message comes from the idea of carpet time. You know, the time when students sit on the carpet and go over our calendar, say the names of the days of the week, count straws to represent what day it is, and go over other routine stuff like that.

In the Morning Message, we take calendar time ideas like the letter, word, number, or skill of the day/week and package it into an engaging Seesaw activity for students to complete. Each of these skills gets a page on the activity. Students start with a letter or the day, which eventually turns into using Little Random Emoji Writing for a word of the day. The number of the day becomes a mini, or

Ben

As a kindergarten teacher, I tried doing carpet time, but I would always get stuck on accountability, meaning that I felt not all my students were engaged in their learning when I did this. Plus, some students seem to completely tune out no matter how hard I tried to engage them.

simplified, MathRep, in which students follow a familiar format to demonstrate their knowledge. Finally, students may complete a Fast and Curious to demonstrate their knowledge of sight words.

Ben's current iteration of the Morning Message came out of necessity while students were at home during shelter in place. Doing calendar time was way harder online, but some of the familiarity of it seemed to be beneficial for students. So it made sense to modify carpet time to a more digital form. This way students got some of the routine practice, but all students were engaged since it was being recorded in Seesaw. After a few different iterations of the Morning Message, it finally dawned on us (or really it dawned on Ben) that the Morning Message was a combination of Emoji Writing, MathReps, and a self-paced version of Fast and Curious.

We call this sequence of different EduProtocols combined in one lesson a Rack and Stack.

Ben's Morning Message Rack and Stack Masters

tinyurl.com/benmorningmessage

Morning Message with Emoji Writing, MathReps, and Fast and Curious

If you check out the image example above, you can see a few different EduProtocols in here, and they are all encompassed in one Seesaw activity. First, we start out with Emoji Writing. In this example, students need to write three different words centered around one emoji. They also have to segment and blend each of the words as

> **Marlena**
>
> Don't worry about the terms "Rack and Stack" or "Stacking," just know that you can combine similar or different EduProtocols to create powerful lesson sequences!

well as say sentences using the words. The next two pages are what we call mini MathReps. In these reps, we focus on number bonds, number sentences, and counting to twenty. Finally, the last part of the activity focuses on the self-paced FAC. We have ten different levels of sight words in this activity. Students watch a video, which reviews the level of sight words for them, then they go over to Quizizz and put in a rep of FAC.

In person, this whole activity takes about thirty minutes. First, we review the word/letter of the day as well as the number of the day. This is done via a Google Slides show. Then, we move to Partner Talk and sharing. We discuss possible words we can write down to repre-

> **Ben**
>
> The Morning Message Rack and Stack is not for beginners. It takes a while to build up to it, but it also shows you the possibilities of Racking and Stacking EduProtocols.

Ben's Morning Message Rack and Stack Masters

Google Slide example of word and number of the day.

sent the emoji. We break the words into syllables and segments. We share sentences using the words. For the number of the day, we discuss how students visualize the number, what the groups are made up of, or what the number sentence would be to represent the number. The questions really change depending on how much time we have and also what skill we are focusing on at the time.

Once students are done discussing the emoji/image and number, we move into the Seesaw activity. If pages are new, or students are having trouble with a portion of the morning message, I open Seesaw and model this portion of the activity in front of students. If students are comfortable with the components of the morning message, then they go open their computer and get going. I put up a twenty-minute timer and walk around the room, touching base with students who need extra help and giving feedback to students as they progress through the activity pages.

As mentioned above, this activity really changes and progresses throughout the year. We start out with a letter of the day and number of the day, and as the students master each section, we push them ahead to the next one. It has also progressed over the years. You can check out all the goodness at tinyurl.com/morningmessagetemp. I run the Morning Message three times a week (Monday, Wednesday, Friday), and it is the first activity we do when students enter the classroom.

*Little Random Emoji Writing + Little p*ARTS*

Little Random Emoji Writing uses random emojis to help students write words, sentences, or paragraphs. In Little p*ARTS, students use an image or video, along with a graphic organizer, to generate different parts of speech to match the media given. Students then put the different parts of speech together to write a sentence or paragraph, using the different parts of speech. In this rack and stack, we combine these two superpowerful EduProtocols for some awesome sentence writing!

As you may have read in our Little Random Emoji Writing chapter, Ben typically runs that EduProtocol with his kindergartners by having them practice writing words instead of writing sentences.

Ben

I use the Quizizz as practice and then try to assess students on Friday to see if they are ready for the next level. I have a classroom aide, which helps me with this, but you could always just use the FAC assessment on Friday to see if they are ready.

Jenn

Notice that they are using one emoji but coming up with three different words. That shows there is not one right answer. That emoji can be a lot of things.

Jenn

You might find that there are some students who do need more support with this activity. What's great about EduProtocols is most students will get independent quickly, which allows you to help those students who need more support in a small-group instruction.

> **Ben & Jenn**
>
> We always love to see people trying out EduProtocols. If you are on X, you can tag us: @Techy_Jenn and @cogswell_ben. And don't forget to tag @EduProtocols and add #EduProtocols as well!

> **Ben**
>
> Remember you can keep progressing through the different Little p*ARTS templates with this Rack and Stack.

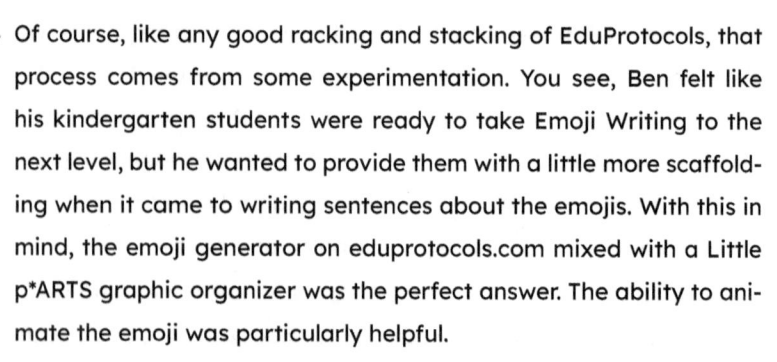

Of course, like any good racking and stacking of EduProtocols, that process comes from some experimentation. You see, Ben felt like his kindergarten students were ready to take Emoji Writing to the next level, but he wanted to provide them with a little more scaffolding when it came to writing sentences about the emojis. With this in mind, the emoji generator on eduprotocols.com mixed with a Little p*ARTS graphic organizer was the perfect answer. The ability to animate the emoji was particularly helpful.

With this EduProtocol, all you have to do is bring up the Random Emoji Power Paragraph generator, turn on "animate emojis," and spin the emojis. Then, using the Little p*ARTS template, you discuss each part of speech as related to the emoji. Ask students, "What noun—what person, place, or thing—do you see here? What is the noun doing, or what is the action?" Using these questions, we generate the different parts of speech in the protocol. One thing to keep in mind is that with kindergarten students we are not connecting the sentences into full paragraphs, but just practicing writing sentences in general.

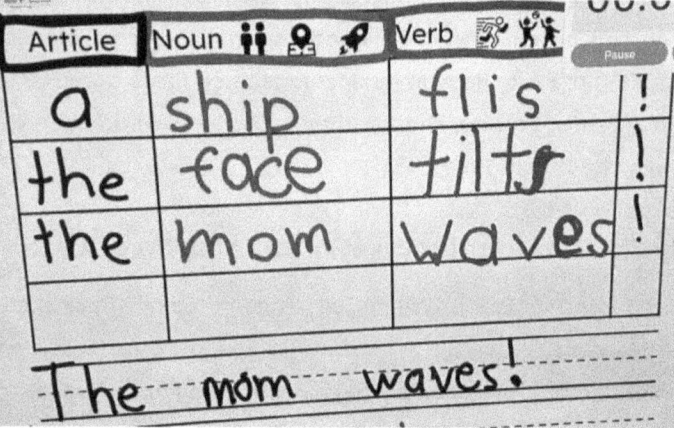

Generate emojis for Little p*ARTS.

Students love to watch as the wheel spins and the emojis pop up. They get to discuss with their partner what noun or verb they see, and then as a class we decide which one we want to write. At the end, they can choose one or two of their favorite sentences and write them down. This whole protocol takes about twenty to thirty minutes, depending how much Partner Talk or phonics practice you want to work into the protocol.

Mix Master

Remember, racking and stacking EduProtocols is about experimentation. It is important to keep the key components to each protocol, but then you can tweak or combine them to enhance student instruction. We encourage you to think about your own ways to rack and stack these different EduProtocols and share them with us as you explore on your journey.

Racking and Stacking EduProtocols Resources

tinyurl.com/StackingFolder

Racking and Stacking EduProtocols Student Examples

tinyurl.com/stackingexamples

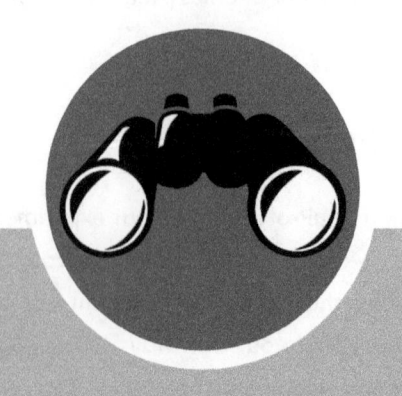

SECTION 4
Smart Start EduProtocols

Chapter 14
Smart Start: Fast and Curious EduProtocol

Now that you have a better idea about what the EduProtocols are, we are going to jump back into Smart Start. In the first Smart Start section, we gave a week at a glance plan of the EduProtocols, and now we are going to dive deeper into exactly what these protocols could look like at the beginning of the year. Fast and Curious (FAC) is one of the easiest EduProtocols to get started with in the primary classroom. As described in chapter 10, with FAC you quickly use a digital assessment tool that is gamified, reteach-related content based on results, and then play again to increase mastery of the content. This process can be done with tons of different content and subjects. So why not get started with it right away, as part of Smart Start, and offer your students a fun way to get to know their teacher and the rest of the class?

A quiz tool, such as Quizizz or Gimkit, works beautifully for Fast and Curious as part of Smart Start. You can also use Blooket, 99Math, or Wordwall—really, any assessment program in which you can add images (and audio as a bonus) will work.

Get to Know the Teacher

One of our favorite ways to start using Fast and Curious in the Smart Start model is to use it to help students get to know the teacher. With FAC, there's no need to spend hours on a handout that no one may read or a fancy Google Slides show. Just create an online quiz about yourself with about 5-10 questions using your favorite digital tool.

Ben & Jenn
You can jump back to chapter 7 to review the Smart Start: Week at a Glance.

Marlena
Practice over time is an effective method in mastering certain content that simply needs to be memorized.

Jenn
My favorite question to ask students is what my favorite candy is because most students also love candy and can then share about their favorite kind. By the way, the answer is Almond Joy.

> **Ben**
>
> My favorite question to ask students is what my favorite color is. It's simple, but everyone connects with it. Of course, most students don't get it right the first time around. So what is my favorite color? Purple, of course.

> **Jenn**
>
> We usually don't get our devices until day 2 or 3 of school, so we will run this protocol very similar to Ben's way if we don't have devices.

> **Jon**
>
> I love Gimkit here because students practice the questions over and over for a set amount of time, and it's so fun!

It is fun to make the questions a variety of some personal and some work-related topics. For example, you might ask your students how many years you have been teaching and also when your birthday is.

After you create the quiz, it is time to run the EduProtocol. This can be done in a variety of ways based on your grade level and preference.

Ben's Way (Kindergarten)

If your classroom is like mine, kindergarten students don't necessarily have devices on day one. Oftentimes, other grades are a priority, which is understandable. Plus, most kindergarten students don't have experience with computers.

With both of these limitations in mind, I start this protocol with the whole group. I start with about five questions for the first quiz, but I may add more as the week progresses. A lot of this depends on the attention span of the class. I keep my questions simple and use images as much as I can. Here are some examples of the questions I use.

- Which one of these is your teacher?
- What is Mr. C's favorite color?
- How many pets does Mr. C have?
- What is Mr. C's favorite food?
- What is Mr. C's favorite number?
- How many children does Mr. C have?

To begin, I open the quiz on my teacher computer, and we play it together as a class. This is a great time to take the opportunity to start reinforcing classroom routines. We start with norms for how to respond to the quiz. Typically, I just have students hold up their fingers to indicate if the answer is 1, 2, 3, or 4. Later, I might have students write their answer choice with numbers on a whiteboard, as this is a great way to teach writing these numbers. Since students tend to get excited, we also take this opportunity to discuss how to

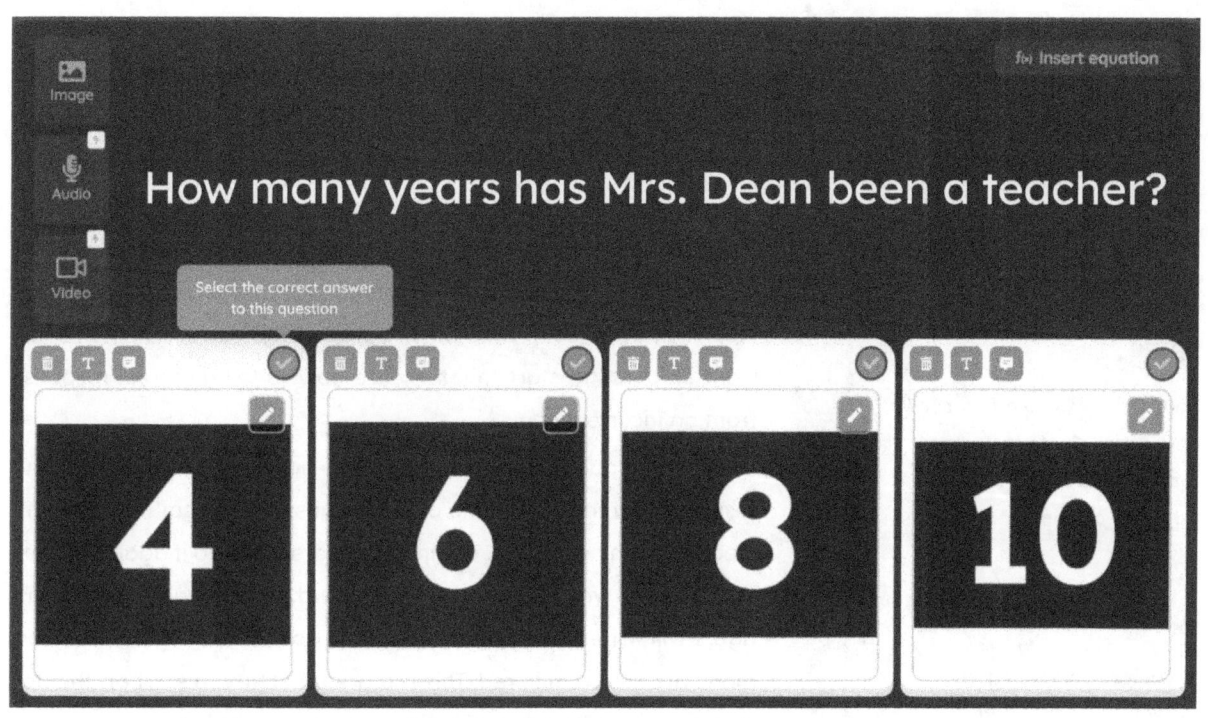

Chapter 14 | Smart Start: Fast and Curious EduProtocol | 143

A Fast and Curious about Mrs. Dean

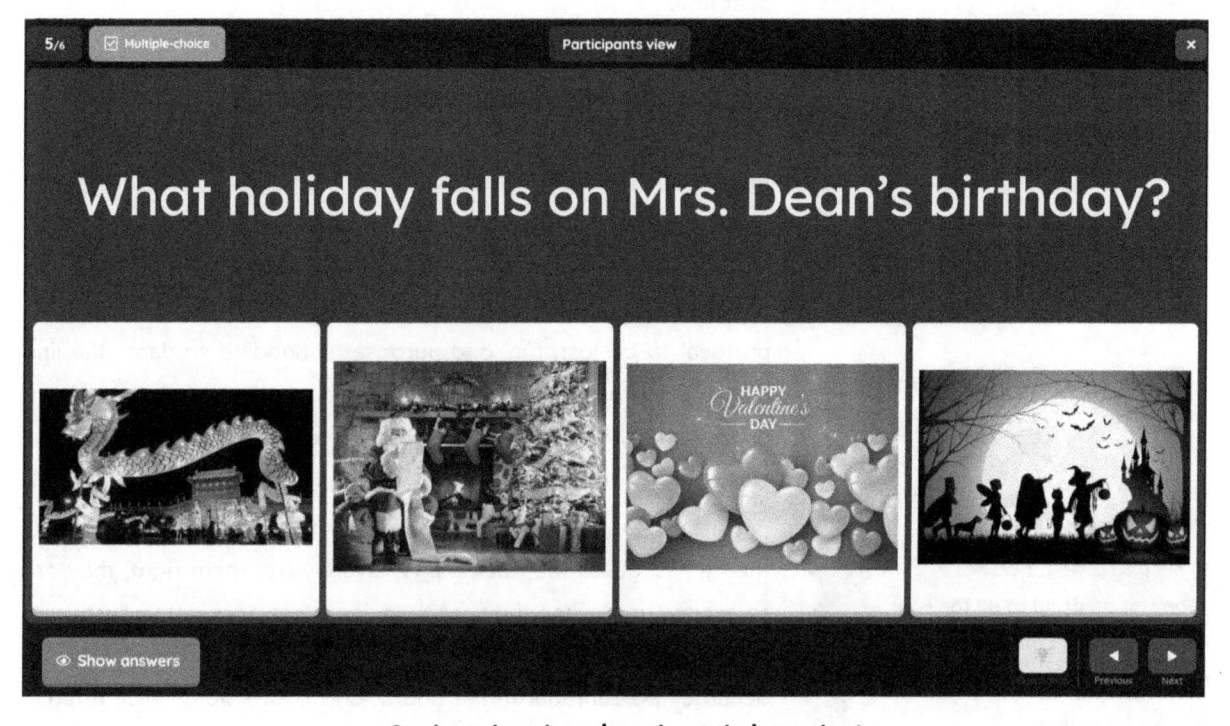

Students love learning about their teacher!

> **Ben**
>
> Another option to get students to respond is to go through the answers one at a time and stand up on the answer they think is correct.

> **Jenn**
>
> You could also do a four corners game. Go to the corner for the answer you think it is. So many options.

> **Ben**
>
> If you are connected to parents, you can send this quiz home for them to do with their students.

> **Jenn**
>
> In second grade, I do not need this scaffold at all for most students, but I can still provide it for those students who do need it.

answer without getting rowdy. Once we start, I won't move on to the next question until everyone shows me they are ready to learn.

With that, we go through the FAC assessment one question at a time. I read the questions and students' responses out loud. With each question, I look around the class to see which answer choice is the most popular, and then we select that choice as a group. After we respond, I take a moment to point out if the answer is correct or incorrect, but I don't take time to review the correct answer. I just want students to start to internalize how to tell a correct response from an incorrect one.

After the quiz is done, we will review how we did. We go over our results, spending more time on which answers we got incorrect. Instead of running the FAC again immediately, we do it again the next day. I like to write the score on the board, but instead of a percentage, I will write how many questions we got correct in green and how many are incorrect in red. This is a great activity to start off the day and get students engaged in their learning. Usually by the third day, we are at 100 percent and we can look back at how we improved over time.

Jenn's Way (1st-2nd)

When I run Fast and Curious as part of Smart Start, I run the assessment as a live quiz. Since this is Smart Start, I always copy the link to the live quiz and send it to my students through Seesaw (or Google Classroom or any other learning management system). I want this protocol to be fast, fun, and purposeful. Sending students the link makes the process much faster and ensures that all students have access and that students do not have to enter any type of game code or type any links.

Once we're in, we play. I love watching the students' reactions as they try to guess the answers. When they get them right, they are so excited, and when they get them incorrect, they act so surprised. After we play the assessment once, we look at the data. I write the accuracy percentage on the board, and then I do a quick reteach based on the data.

Score	Points Out of 45	Q1 45%	Q2 58%	Q3 65%	Q4 58%	Q5 55%	Q6 35%
8860	45 (100%)	✓	✓	✓	✓	✓	✓
8710	45 (100%)	✓	✓	✓	✓	✓	✓
8200	45 (100%)	✓	✓	✓	✓	✓	✓
8120	45 (100%)	✓	✓	✓	✓	✓	✓
9680	40 (89%)	✓	✓	✓	✓	✓	✗
7180	40 (89%)	✓	✓	✓	✓	✗	✓
6890	40 (89%)	✓	✗	✓	✓	✓	✓
6710	40 (89%)	✓	✗	✓	✓	✓	✓
8450	35 (78%)	✓	✓	✓	!	✓	✗
7670	35 (78%)	✗	✓	✓	✓	✓	✗
7460	35 (78%)	!	✓	✓	✓	!	✓
7340	35 (78%)	✗	✓	✓	✓	✓	✗
7070	35 (78%)	✓	✓	✓	✓	✗	✗
6810	35 (78%)	✗	✓	✓	✓	✓	✗
6460	35 (78%)	✓	✗	✓	✓	✓	✗

Review the questions that students missed while focusing on the correct answers before immediately taking the Fast and Curious quiz again.

Jenn

When we look at this data, what do we see? What questions do I need to focus on the most? Question 6 is definitely the one I want to really solidify with my students.

> **Ben & Jenn**
> Remember, one key to introducing EduProtocols is to do it in a fun, engaging way. This isn't just about getting to know your teacher, but learning FAC.

For the reteach, I show each question and review the answers. I tell students the correct answer and help them remember it. For example, the first question might ask how many years I have been teaching. If the answer is less than ten, I would have students show me the answer with their fingers. Then we would count it out. I would ask them again, "How many years have I been teaching?" Using strategies like these helps students remember when we do the quiz again.

After reteaching based on the data, we immediately play the quiz again. We look at the accuracy percentage again and really emphasize the growth. If need be, I might play again the next day. It all depends on how the first run of the protocol went. The idea of this is to teach the protocol while also building a positive classroom culture. The students get to know their teacher and the protocol at the same time. The next step is getting to know each other using the same protocol.

Get to Know Each Other

> **Ben**
> When we start this activity, we still do it as a whole group. At this point, I like to have students come up and lead the activity. Once students are ready and we have devices, I can then send the quiz to them in Seesaw.

After students have used Fast and Curious to get to know you, their teacher, they can use it to get to know each other. In chapter 4, we explained the importance of students learning each other's names to build a safe, welcoming, and productive classroom culture. Fast and Curious can help the students achieve that goal.

Start by taking your students' pictures. Use an online quiz platform to add their pictures as answer options. For the assessment question, show a student's picture and then ask the group to supply their name. The answers can be done in audio or text format. The students then pick the picture of the correct student. We like to do five or six students as the answer options (depending on class size). This way, all you have to do to build the quiz is to duplicate the question and change the student's name and the correct answer. This is also helpful because students are only practicing five or six names a day instead of the entire class. Each day of the week, we do a different group of students until the class has had a chance to practice each student's name.

> **Jenn**
> A fun option is pulling each student over one at a time and having them record their own name. This way everyone knows exactly how to say each name correctly.

Just as we did with the iteration above, we can look at the data regarding how students have gotten to know each other. We can see which student names the majority of the class is struggling with. When we reteach, we reteach with all students but really emphasize the names that the class needs more practice with.

For more practice, students whose names the class is struggling with stand up and tell us something about themselves. We can all practice writing their name on a whiteboard or say the letters aloud together. After reteaching, run the protocol again. See the growth. By doing this, you are not only reteaching but making all students feel welcome and creating a positive culture.

Ben

I like to create one quiz with all the students first, and then copy it and delete the questions until I have just five or six students.

Ben & Jenn

Why not use another EduProtocol to help? We like to look and see which students we need to get to know more and pick those students for Sketch and Tell.

Using Fast and Curious to learn classmates' names is fun and efficient and allows the teacher to spot students having difficulty learning the names of their peers.

Get to Know the Class

After students have had a week of practicing five or six student names a day, the next step is to compile the list to really get to know the class. This takes a little bit longer because the number of questions increases.

However, when we do this, instead of doing the traditional model of FAC where we do the quiz, reteach, and then do the quiz again, we assign this as an asynchronous assignment. This way, students play the FAC on their own until they get at least a 90 percent. After two weeks of Fast and Curious, all students will know each other's names! The best part is that you, as the teacher, can still see the data and see if there are some students who still don't know the names, or if there are some names most students are struggling with. You can then take those students and reteach during your morning message.

> **Jenn**
>
> I will even work with students in a small group with the pictures of students they were struggling with. I also like to give rewards for learning names.

Chapter 15
Smart Start: Sketch and Tell EduProtocol

Sketch and Tell, as discussed in chapter 12, seems simple on the surface: you sketch an idea, and you then tell about it. However, as with all of the EduProtocols, we like to introduce Sketch and Tell in a low-cognitive way. This is why we love using this one in the beginning of the year. Introduce this protocol on day one of school. Explain to students that they are going to get to know each other by sketching a self-portrait and telling details about themselves. This builds class community in a seamless way.

Of course, you will need to explain what a self-portrait is, but the idea is to give students time to draw themselves. Self-portraiture is something all students can do because it does not require any background knowledge; they have their own ideas of themselves and can draw immediately. When they are done, they can tell details about themselves. However, in kindergarten we do this a little differently.

Ben & Jenn
Want to do a deep dive in Sketch and Tell? Check out chapter 12.

Jon
Do six to eight Sketch and Tells on paper, then you can slide Seesaw or Nearpod right in. Easy-peasy!

Ben's Way (Kindergarten)

I like to begin by modeling Sketch and Tell instead of just having students start drawing. Some kindergarten students have not used a pencil or crayon before or do not have a lot of experience with sketching. Therefore, in kindergarten, I have the students draw their first self-portrait by following along with me.

For example, when I draw my face, I would model drawing the oval and using the word *oval*, asking the students if they could draw an oval for their face too. Then I ask students, "What color should I

Ben

If you can get your hands on some Colors of the World crayons, these are super helpful when having students draw themselves.

Ben & Jenn

Representation matters, and having a variety of colors for students to use is essential. Just as Ben said, if you can get some Colors of the World crayons do it!

Ben

Even though I pretend to pick randomly, I like to try to pick more outgoing or confident students first.

Marlena

I like interviewing students and then creating a shared writing about that child so we can read it again and again as a class.

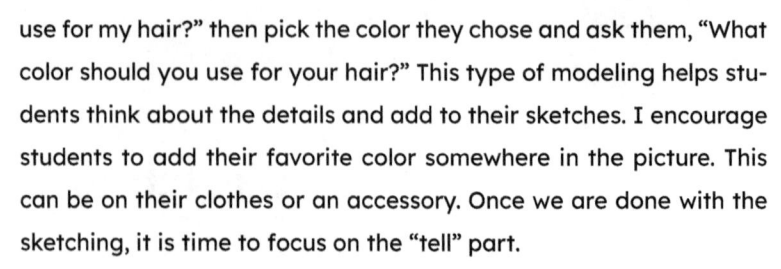

use for my hair?" then pick the color they chose and ask them, "What color should you use for your hair?" This type of modeling helps students think about the details and add to their sketches. I encourage students to add their favorite color somewhere in the picture. This can be on their clothes or an accessory. Once we are done with the sketching, it is time to focus on the "tell" part.

In kindergarten, asking students to write on the first day of school is not only scary but can also give kids lots of anxiety. Instead, I ask them to think about what they want to tell about themselves. This is not as easy as you might think, because students in kindergarten may not have a lot of experience with language, so they might not be sure how to tell about themselves. Students are also very shy at the beginning of the year, so I start small with just two questions: "What is your name?" and "What is your favorite color?" At the same time, I encourage students to think about other things they know about themselves as well.

After the students are done with drawing, I collect their pictures. Then, throughout the day for the next few days, I will pick a student and have them come up and tell about themselves. After they share their name and favorite color in a complete sentence, I ask them if there is anything else they want to say about themselves. I like to do this every time we transition to the carpet, as it gets students used to presenting to their classmates right away. I also like to use these opportunities to reinforce active listening to students.

Besides having students Sketch and Tell about themselves, I like to introduce Directed Drawing and build some of the sketching and coloring skills. Because we are the Kinder Rockets, I like to start with my space theme.

A rocket can be easily drawn with simple shapes like rectangles, triangles, and circles. On Day 1, we will draw a rocket on paper. We talk about what coloring vs. scribbling looks like, and I provide a few models. Then the next day, if we have computers, we will draw a rocket in Seesaw and record ourselves telling about it. Flip-flopping between paper and digital not only helps build drawing skills but builds digital skills as well.

A beginning Directed Drawing lesson in Seesaw to help students connect to the theme of our classroom

Ben & Jenn

With paper drawings, we don't always take the time to tell about our pictures in the beginning because students may not be ready for Partner Talk. However, we do encourage students to record themselves telling about their Seesaw drawing as soon as possible.

Jenn's Way (1st-2nd)

Modeling how to sketch a self-portrait is an effective way to teach students how to Sketch and Tell without pressure. It also helps to build culture, showing how we are all individuals who make up a classroom community.

When I introduce Sketch and Tell, I usually hand students a template, which is just a piece of paper that has the word *sketch* on one side and *tell* on the other.

Ben

Once students are ready for Partner Talk procedures, I have them share about their Directed Drawings as much as they can.

Sketch	Tell

The basic Sketch and Tell template format

Ben & Jenn

That's another easy feature about using Seesaw. Students can tell right away just by recording their voice.

Then I tell students we are going to sketch ourselves. I like to model my own self-portrait first to help the students who need it, while also encouraging others to add more details. I do this very similarly to Ben. I ask the kids what color I should use for my hair, my eyes, what kind of clothes I can add, and all sorts of things to help them create their own self-portrait. The way we do the sketch is very similar; the difference is in how we tell.

In first grade, writing is very challenging in the beginning. As a result, you should encourage students to write details using keywords. For example, maybe one detail is that a student is six years old. They can just write the word *six* or even draw that number. But there are other details they can add. For example, one detail we want to share is our names, so I have students add their names to the "tell" side. This writing can be differentiated, too. So ask students to write their first and last name if they can, or use their name plates to help them.

Another thing I like to do is teach students how to use their color words. In my classroom, we have a blue folder (a folder with resources like sight words, color words, days of the week, etc.) that is our helping folder. In this folder, there are color words to tell them how to spell the names of colors. To help them with the tell side, I ask the same questions Ben does, but I teach them how to find the color words to tell about their hair or eyes. For example, if they say their eyes are brown, I ask them to find the color brown and write that word on the "tell" side.

This helps students write a couple details, even if they are just one-word details. It also helps them learn how to use their blue folder of helpful resources, which I use a lot in first grade.

> **Jenn**
>
> I also have them write with that color. One, they get to use more colors, which they love, and two, it helps them to "read" what they wrote when they tell their partners about themselves.

> **Jenn**
>
> Give students a time frame. If you just let them go, some students will take twenty minutes, and others will be done in two minutes. Telling students they have exactly five minutes to complete one side helps to make this EduProtocol run much smoother.

> **Jon**
>
> Teach them to finish. It is a skill they will use their whole life!

A completed Sketch and Tell about Mrs. Dean

In second grade, I do not model the portrait so much. Instead, I simply teach students what a self-portrait is, and I tell them they have a certain amount of time to sketch their own.

As students are working, I walk around the room and ask them questions so that they will add details. When it comes to the "tell" part, students can write specific details about themselves right away. You can also differentiate this easily by telling students to write as many details as they can in five minutes (or whatever time frame you want to give them, depending on the needs of your students the first time you introduce this). This is more so that when they get a chance to "tell," they have notes to help them.

Ben & Jenn

Remember to have students share with a partner in between sketching and writing. This makes the writing process go smoother and can be easily done at the beginning of second grade.

A Sketch and Tell about Mrs. Dean using complete sentences

After students have completed their sketches and their notes, they take turns sharing in their groups. In this example, students are practicing the EduProtocol while also getting to know each other, which is so important in the beginning of the school year.

Second graders can have even more fun with this EduProtocol. After students share their sketches and notes, you can take this to the next level and have them work as a group to create one Sketch and Tell. On the "sketch" side, students can add their original sketches. They can just glue them onto the "sketch" side. Then on the "tell" side, students work together to write either the details they had in common or one detail for each person. Then the whole

> **Ben & Jenn**
>
> This particular version is better for second grade. In kindergarten and first grade, we just want students practicing sketching and telling, but in second grade, students can take it to the next level by creating their group Sketch and Tell.

class can practice telling about their sketches quickly. That way, the entire class has two ways to practice this EduProtocol while getting to know each other.

Other Prompts

The self-portrait is one of our favorite ways to introduce Sketch and Tell, but we have a lot of others we also enjoy Smart Start-ing with. Some of our favorites include:

- What is something that makes you happy?
- What is an activity you enjoy?
- Who is in your family?
- What kind of pet would you like to have?
- What is your favorite color? How many things can you sketch that are that color?

Modify the "tell" side based on your grade level or class readiness.

| The Sketch Part || The Tell Part ||
Prompt	Sketch	Share	Tell
What is something that makes you happy? Or what are some things that make you happy?	Either sketch one thing that makes you happy or a few things.	Explain your drawing to your partner or record about it in Seesaw.	K: write the letter sound it starts with 1: label each thing 2: write 2-4 sentences about what makes you happy

The flow of a Sketch and Tell: Prompt, sketch, pair share, and tell (the writing).

What is a skill that all students need to complete this protocol? Sketching! We know that in the TK–2 classroom, drawing is essential for so many reasons. In fact, it is most likely one of your go-to activities. Draw a picture of something that starts with the letter A. Draw a picture of your family. Draw a picture of your dream pet. However, many students in kindergarten come into the classroom with little to no experience with drawing materials. In all the grades, there may also be a lack of vocabulary in regard to what things they know of to sketch. For example, if you want to sketch things that start with the letter A, students may not have a lot of vocabulary or ideas of things that start with that letter. Additionally, students are all over the place in their ability to draw digitally, as well as on paper. This is why we think it is so important to introduce the skills required to Sketch and Tell immediately. So how do we start? Directed Draw and Tell!

Variation: Directed Draw and Tell

You may have read the section on Directed Drawing in chapter 4. Therefore, you may already know that Directed Drawing is a tool that guides students on the steps needed to complete a specific drawing. Thanks to the internet, there are TONS of resources to find videos to help with Directed Drawing. You can look up almost anything you want to draw. Since Directed Drawing is a way to introduce Sketch and Tell, we like to do Directed Drawings that are directly related to the Sketch and Tell that we want to complete.

For example, in the beginning of the school year, one of our favorite books to read is *How the Crayons Saved the School*. In this book, students learn that we need all the colors to make school a great place to be. To connect this book to our Directed Drawing, we ask the students, "What is something that has all the colors?" Usually at least one student, if not more, can come up with the answer: a rainbow. Then we pull up a Directed Drawing video on making a rainbow. We draw the rainbow as a class. We pause the video for each step so students can follow along as we model on their own paper under the document camera (or on the whiteboard). Then students get to color their rainbow.

Jenn

Even in first grade, I always have at least one student who does not know how to write their name or have experience coloring with different materials. I have to teach them how to hold a crayon to scribble, then draw, then write.

Ben & Jenn

During this time, students are also learning how to follow multistep directions, use materials, and gain the skills needed to do this protocol completely independently.

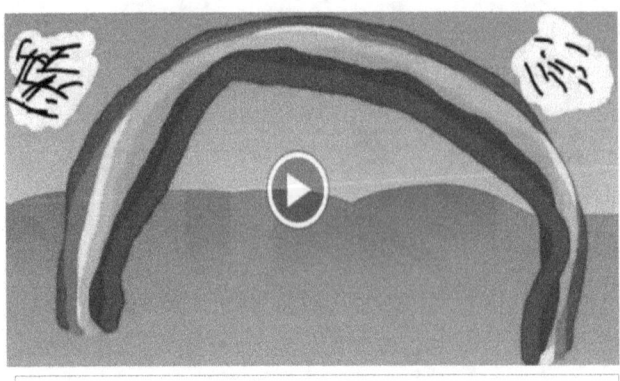

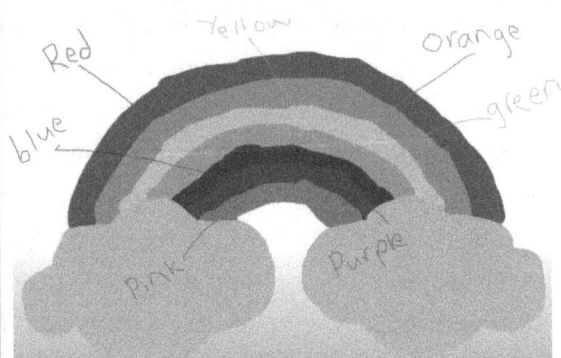

156 | The EduProtocol Field Guide Primary Edition

| Kindergarten Example | First Grade Example |

A kindergarten and first grade sample of a Directed Drawing rainbow

The "tell" side can be done in so many different ways. It's super easy to modify based on the needs of your students as well as grade level.

Kindergarten	Students draw the rainbow and name the colors in the rainbow.
First Grade	Students draw the rainbow and label the colors they used to tell about their picture.
Second Grade	Students draw the rainbow and write two to four sentences to tell about their picture independently.

Ben

I like to teach students the rainbow song: "Red, orange, yellow, green, followed by blue, indigo, and violet. That's the rainbow song for you."

Ben

I like to try to do a Directed Drawing every day for the first week. I try to squeeze it in every day during weeks 2 and 3 as well, but I don't always have time.

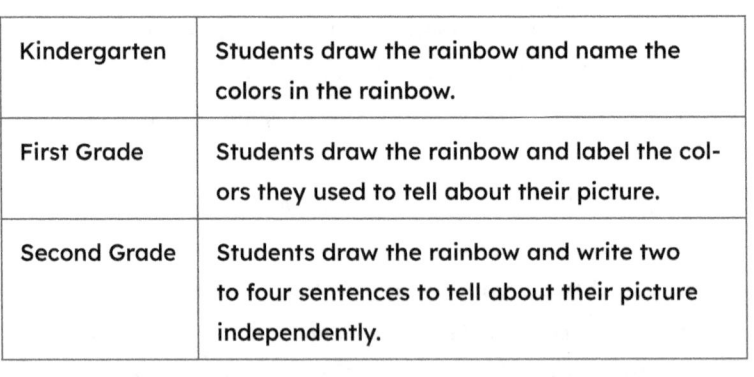

In each example, students "tell" verbally. This gets kids talking. We like to do this about two to three times per week the first month of school to really get students to master the skills needed for Sketch and Tell.

Sometimes spending time with Directed Drawing can feel like a waste of academic class time or just another thing to squeeze in. However, there are big payoffs in the long run. With several Directing Drawing sessions for practice, students are able to sketch quickly and with so much more detail. Also, keep in mind that Directed Drawing is a great way to build in the names of shapes because so many things can be drawn with simple shapes. Lastly, use Directed Drawing as an opportunity to enrich the students' vocabulary as you are drawing as well. The richer our vocabulary is, the richer the students' vocabulary will be.

Ben & Jenn

Don't feel like it's a waste of time. There are so many skills being taught in Directed Drawing time, and the trick is to connect it to what you are learning standards wise.

Directed Drawing Resources

tinyurl.com/directeddrawresources

Chapter 16
Smart Start: MathReps EduProtocol

MathReps.com

MathReps Folder

tinyurl.com/
MathRepsfolder

Ben & Jenn

Learn more about mastering MathReps in chapter 11.

As we explored in chapter 11, MathReps are a quick, effective, way to practice and perfect several mathematical skills and standards simultaneously. To review, through MathReps, students complete a math mat (usually a series of questions on a wipeable surface), which typically covers multiple skills and standards. Over several reps, students keep completing the MathReps until they reach mastery on key concepts. Then the MathRep might change or morph to incorporate new skills, but it will often keep previous skills as well.

With MathReps, we spiral skills throughout the year so that students review, retain, and remember mathematical concepts with ease. MathReps can be done on paper or digitally, and, as part of Smart Start, they can be quickly introduced at the beginning of the year.

We especially love to use MathReps in our Smart Start because of the simple format. They have a low cognitive entry point but build a strong number sense, which is the foundation for our TK–2 learners. They also are an excellent replacement for something many TK–2 teachers already utilize: the number of the day in their calendar system. Using the MathRep every day for the number of the day helps students focus on those foundational skills and get more and more repetition. By the end of the first week, students are becoming MathRep pros.

Chapter 16 | Smart Start: MathReps EduProtocol | 159

Ben's Way (Kindergarten)

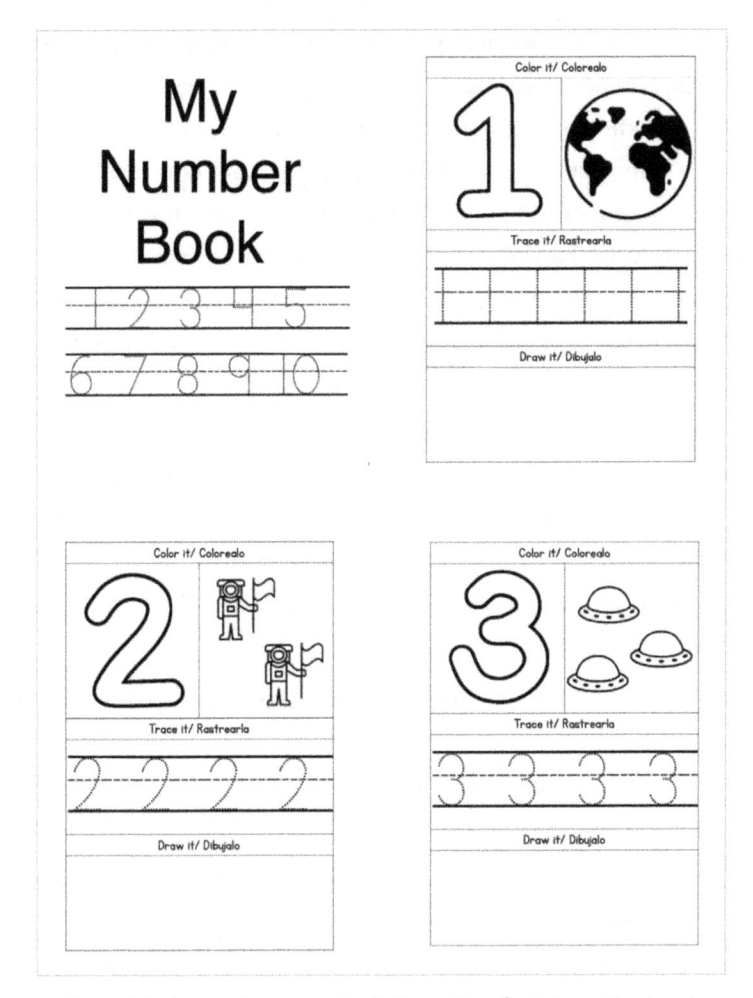

Start kindergartners on MathReps the first day of school with this mini MathRep booklet.

I love to start MathReps on day one because they allow me to reinforce many skills, like number sense, number recognition, fine motor skills, penmanship, drawing, and coloring. I don't start with a full-blown MathRep, but a mini MathRep called "My Number Booklet." This is an eleven-page book with a cover followed by a page for each number 1–10. On each page, students color the number, color a number of objects to match a number, trace the number, and then draw items to represent the number. We go through the numbers, one at

Ben and Jenn's MathReps Activities and Resources

tinyurl.com/k-2mathreps

Ben's MathReps Booklet Resource

tinyurl.com/mathrepbooklet

Links to Ben and Jenn's Seesaw MathReps

tinyurl.com/seesawMathRep

Ben

If you look at the example image, each page has a brief instruction in English and in Spanish. After we do the number in class, I like to send the page home for students to complete with their family.

> **Jenn**
>
> Notice how much modeling goes into this. It is important to help reinforce the skills. Model, model, model. This will help when you dive into it more for independent time.

> **Ben**
>
> This is a great opportunity to work on class choral responses. When it's my turn, I point my open hand to my chest. When it's the students' turn, I gesture my hand to the class and have them answer. We also talk about answering in a complete sentence. It takes some time, but why not start it on day one as an expectation.

> **Ben**
>
> If students get used to feedback on small things like coloring more, then when I ask them to go back and change something in their writing they are less resistant.

a time, over the course of ten days. Repeating these steps for each number constitutes the "reps" for the MathRep.

As with almost everything else in the beginning of kindergarten, I take time to model what goes into each page of "My Number Booklet." I give students coloring tips, focusing on how to use small, short strokes with their crayons, how to stop when they come to a line, how to turn the paper if it makes it easier to color, and how to go back and color over the white spots. We review the correct formation of the numbers, starting from top to bottom, with the goal of making pretty numbers. We trace the number in the air a few times. And finally, we draw an object for them to count with each number.

In the beginning, this object might be something super simple, like one smiley face. I have students share ideas of what they want to draw, reinforcing how we share as active listeners. We go back and count the number of objects we draw to make sure they correspond to the number of the day. We then quickly review each section with questions like:

- Question: What number is this? Echo Response: The number is one.
- Question: How many objects do you see? Echo Response: I see one planet earth.
- Question: How do I draw the number one? Echo Response: I draw the number one from top to bottom.
- Question: How many items did you draw? Echo Response: I drew one smiley face.

After we review the page, it's time to hand out the "My Number Booklets." We make sure to find page one, and we begin working. For the first few days, I leave my version up for students in case they need a reference. I walk around the room, pointing out what students are doing well and giving feedback to students who need to improve on a particular section. I encourage almost every student to go back and color more to get rid of white spots. It may seem like a small thing, but it is a good start to students internalizing, and acting on, feedback from their teacher.

The wireless doc cam is one way to showcase student work to the whole class.

After a student completes their "My Number Booklet," they turn it in, and they can get out their Play-Doh. They use their Play-Doh to make the number of the day or make objects to represent the number one of the day. Once students are finished, I like to take some time to review their work under the document camera. I point out students who did particularly well. I try to give a quick compliment to each student. I also look for overall trends to give feedback on.

This series of activities continues until we are finished with the booklet. As a culminating activity, students make a Seesaw video reviewing each number in their booklet. After the mini MathRep, we are ready to jump into our first full-blown MathRep.

Jon

I routinely walk into first-grade classes and drop a MathRep under the doc cam and say "Copy me." The kids skip right along. Then I have them flip the paper (same MathRep on the other side), and I say "What number should we do next?" They get right to work. I ask kids to come up and do one on the doc cam if they are a fast finisher, so we can check each other's work. I can get kids who don't even know me to do twelve to fifteen problems in under fifteen minutes.

Ben

I love my portable iPevo Wireless document camera because it lets me highlight awesome student work right from their desk.

Jenn

Making something with Play-Doh to show the number is a great introduction to our Build and Tell, which you can read more about in chapter 12.

Ben

Another option when students are done is to have students make a video in Seesaw explaining what they did on their number of the day.

Marlena

What makes the little booklet a MathRep is that it has the same format spread over multiple days, as students are completing only one page a day. Later this will translate to the "number of the day" that they will use to complete the more involved multi-standard MathReps.

Jenn's Way (1st-2nd)

I love starting with MathReps on day one of school because they are a fantastic way to review what students already know while really reinforcing some strong number sense skills. So how do I do it?

Calendar Time MathReps

In first grade, a lot of teachers have a calendar routine in which they teach a lot of mathematical concepts. I do a very modified version of this using the number of the day with MathReps. Instead of doing the traditional calendar time, where students sit on the carpet and count the number of days we have been in school in a variety of ways, we have our digital calendar on our large-format displays. We review the month and days of the week, and then we move the marker to show what our current day is. We review the date, and we review how many days we have been in school. Then, we use the MathReps number of the day for how many days we have been in school.

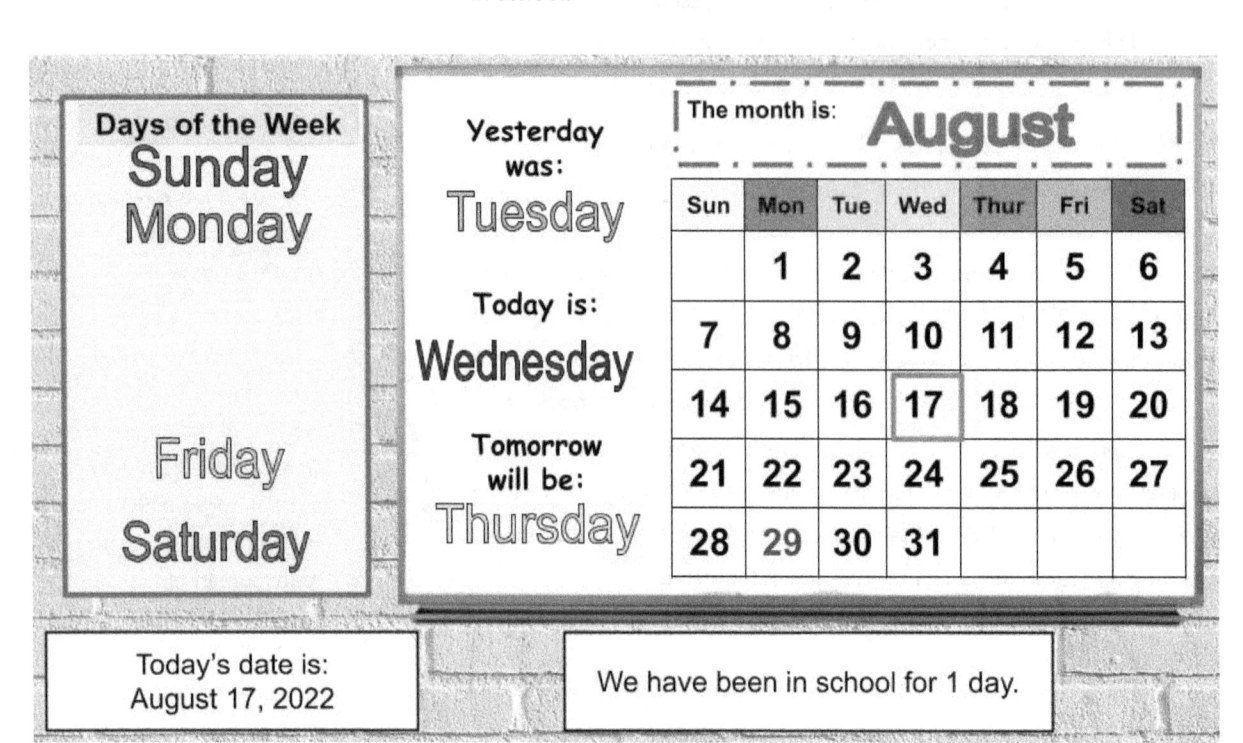

Our digital class calendar

In this example, it is the first day of school, so we have been in school for 1 day. Therefore, we complete the MathRep for the number 1.

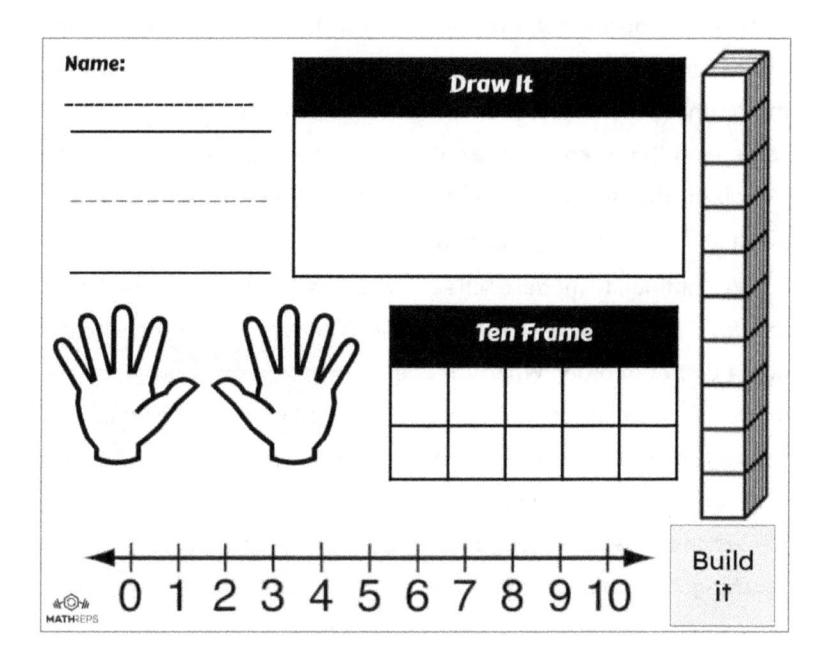

A multi-standard MathRep used during calendar time.

When we do the MathRep, it is very modeled. Similar to Ben, I ask questions with echo responses. For example, I might ask, "How many days have we been in school this year?" and students would reply, telling me one or, "It is our first day." However, one thing I do that is a little different is I start showing students how to use their helping folder.

As mentioned in other chapters, I use a blue folder every year that has helpers for students to learn how to find sight words, color words, days of the week, and so many other important things we use so they can get the help they need immediately. Those tools include numbers, number lines, a hundred chart, and more. Therefore, when I do the number of the day, I also teach students how to use this blue folder to help them. I have them open it up and find the number 1. Then I ask students if any of them can draw the number 1 all by themselves. At this point, I can usually already tell who knows how to do this, and I ask for a helper to model it for us. After they model it, I show them again and ask them to copy along.

Ben

Building student independence from day one is super important. Jenn uses a helping folder to make sure they can find their own resources and build independence.

> **Jenn**
>
> Depending on the class, you could also ask them what toppings we should draw on the pizza and add those details too. The idea is to be constantly building language and getting students sharing even while doing a MathRep.

> **Jenn**
>
> Just as Ben does, we do this for the first ten days of school (or two weeks). It is an amazing review of what they learned in kindergarten, which helps students feel confident. It builds language, it reinforces strong number sense skills, and it teaches them the MathReps protocol so we can really jump into the full-on MathReps.

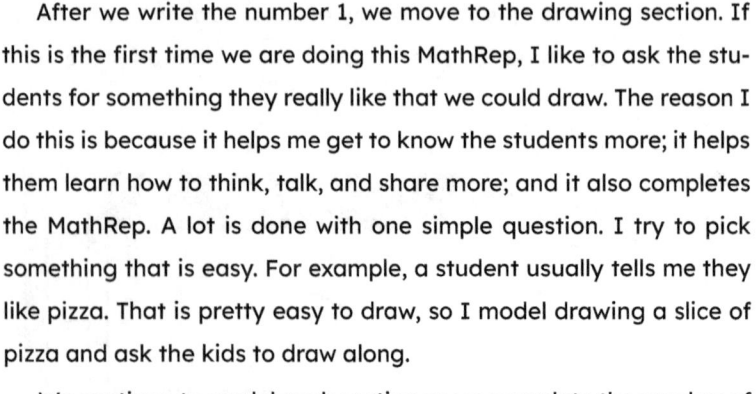

After we write the number 1, we move to the drawing section. If this is the first time we are doing this MathRep, I like to ask the students for something they really like that we could draw. The reason I do this is because it helps me get to know the students more; it helps them learn how to think, talk, and share more; and it also completes the MathRep. A lot is done with one simple question. I try to pick something that is easy. For example, a student usually tells me they like pizza. That is pretty easy to draw, so I model drawing a slice of pizza and ask the kids to draw along.

We continue to model each section as we complete the number of the day. Then the next day, we complete the same sequence with the next number in order. When I model the activity on Day 2, I ask for more help from students. Then I do a quick walk around/glance to see who is getting it and who needs more help. Each day I do this with a little less modeling and more student leading. As we go into the second week of school, I continue with the activity, but I add in teaching students how to the steps of the MathRep digitally as well. For example, in the second week of school, I have students complete the MathRep on paper, but then I show how to take a good picture in Seesaw and record telling about their MathReps. Then the next day I show them how to do the entire MathRep digitally.

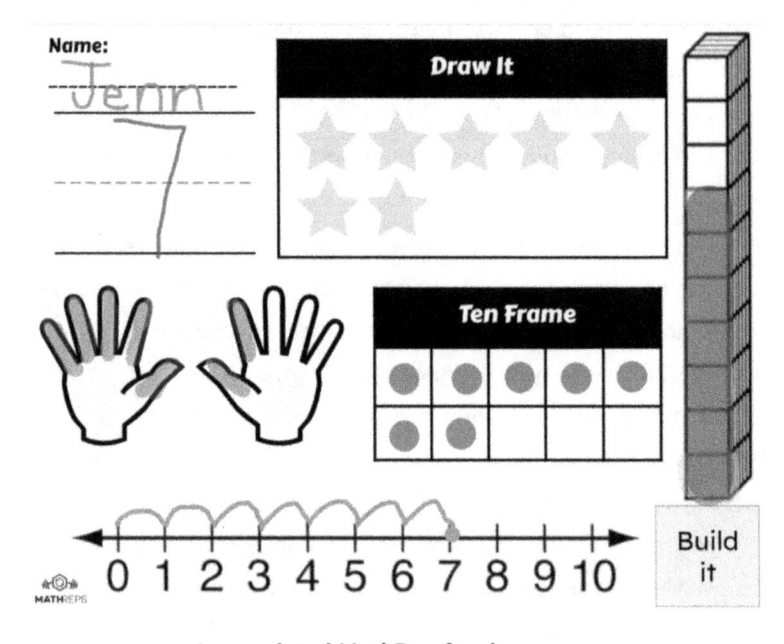

A completed MathRep for day seven.

MathReps with Fast and Curious

In second grade, the above process would be a little too easy and not engaging enough. So I like to jump right into MathReps Smart Start with a first-grade spiral review.

However, before I run MathReps for review, I first run assessments with Fast and Curious. This rack and stack helps me introduce two EduProtocols together. Because students are already familiar with Fast and Curious from the Smart Start variations in chapter 14, the combination with MathReps helps me to reinforce what I've already taught them.

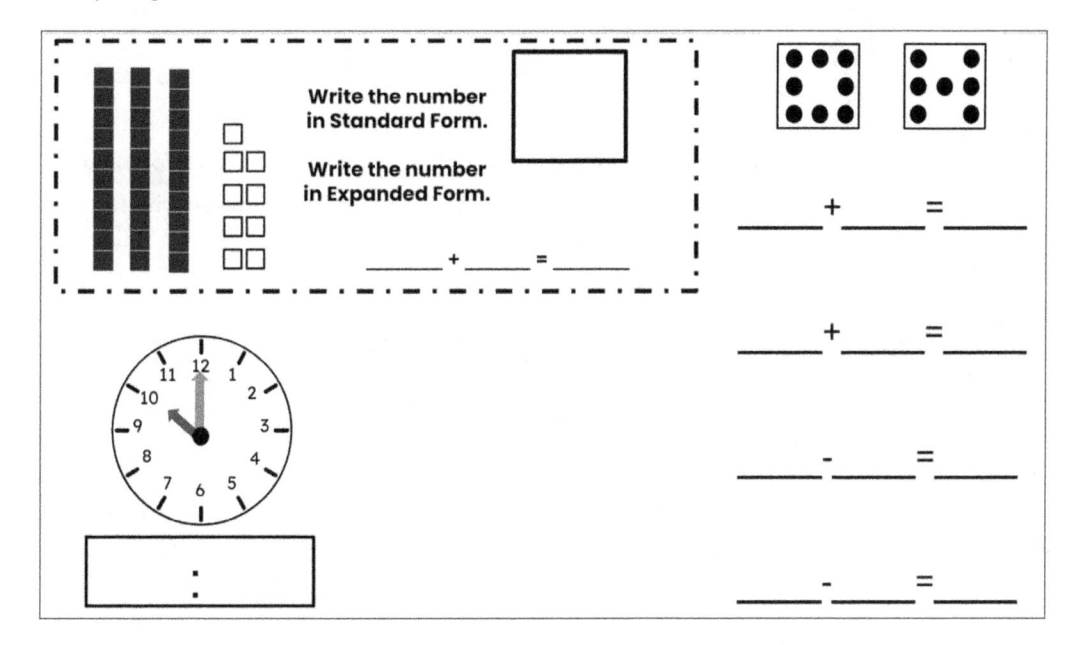

> **Ben & Jenn**
> You can read more about racking and stacking FAC in chapter 13.

First grade spiral review MathReps for second graders

This Smart Start version of MathReps is very modeled. I use it as a teaching time to review many skills that were learned in first grade. Again, this helps students feel confident, because most will know these skills and will need only a little review. I then use the data from the FAC to help me really know which students may need more help and which questions need more time with the teaching part.

For example, when we start with the number in standard form, we count the tens and ones together. Often, I have to stop after the tens and say, "Now we count by ones" and really model, for example, counting 31, 32, 33 (rather than 40, 50, 60) because students tend to still struggle with switching over how they count between tens and ones. Then I review how the standard form is just the number. I will ask the students what number we just counted and review how to write it. We do this for each part. Then we run FAC again to show growth.

Just as in first grade, while we start MathReps on paper for the first week, in the second week I will show students how to complete MathReps digitally as well. After doing this for the first two weeks of school, then we can really go into full-blown MathReps with a lot more independence.

Again, I like to introduce MathReps this way in second grade because students tend to already have a lot of those digital skills we teach in kindergarten and first grade. Moreover, this combination helps to reinforce the FAC EduProtocol in combination with the new element of MathReps.

Start Smart with MathReps

Taking the time to jump into MathReps before your curriculum begins in earnest can really help build students' skills and confidence and can set you up for a year of success. You will see how MathReps grow and change as the year grows on. Build on the MathReps Smart Start, and get into the groove as you transition and increase the complexity and difficulty of the Reps.

Jenn

In second grade, I make this my math lesson for the day. Therefore, instead of doing other math lessons from my curriculum, I use this for the first two weeks of school.

Ben & Jenn

Remember you can go back to chapter 11 to learn more about implementing MathReps, and check out MathReps.com.

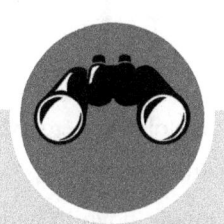

Chapter 17
Final Thoughts and Call to Action

Congratulations on reading *EduProtocols: TK–2 Primary Edition*. We hope we have equipped you with enough knowledge to start with EduProtocols or take your current EduProtocol implementation to the next level. We want to leave you with a few final thoughts on implementing EduProtocols in your classroom.

First, don't feel like you need to try every EduProtocol at once. If you remember in our Smart Start Seesaw chapter, we discuss layering Seesaw skills on one at a time. We suggest doing something similar with EduProtocols. So start with the one EduProtocol that you feel most comfortable with. Then, make sure to find a good spot to add new EduProtocols into your long-term schedule. EduProtocols require consistency and repetition; if you don't have these, then they will not work.

Second, give yourself some grace. There will be bumps along the road to implementation. There is no one straight line to EduProtocol success. We have been implementing and experimenting with EduProtocols for years, and we are still tweaking and adjusting them as we need to. In fact, we tweaked our EduProtocols over the course of writing this book. Each class, and student, is different. Oftentimes things work differently in different settings. The important part is to just keep on trying and adjusting EduProtocols as you need to. Come back to this book as you need to; it's meant to serve as an ongoing reference for you.

Lastly, we are here for you, and so is the community. There are many ways to reach out for support with implementing EduProto-

> **Ben & Jenn**
> Big high five! Thanks for coming along with us on this journey.

> **Jon**
> I spent most of my eighteen classroom years above sixth grade. Primary was a mystery to me. But I've done a bunch of EduProtocols with TK–2 kids in the last two years, and they can totally do these! I've seen kids laughing and cheering about our work after only being with them for fifteen minutes.

cols, including eduprotocols.com, where you can also get free templates, ideas, and fun things like the Random Emoji generator.

With the invention of the internet, we no longer have to be isolated in our teaching. No one needs to teach alone. Even if we are not on the same page as our immediate colleagues, we can always find a teacher friend online who is ready to learn with us. EduProtocols are better together!

> Learn more about what Ben and Jenn are doing at their blog!
>
> tinyurl.com/primaryeduprotocolsblog

> **Ben & Jenn**
> Remember, you can interact with us on X (@Techy_Jenn or @cogswell_ben) or visit our special, hidden EduProtocols Extended Content area on the website.

> **Ben & Jenn**
> Did you know we are also available to come to your school or professional development event?

> **Ben & Jenn**
> Here's the table of contents for our Extended Content one more time: tinyurl.com/eppewebsite Password: 73468.

Extended Content:
Final Thoughts and Call to Action

Final Thoughts and Call to Action included some extra awesome resources and links that you might find helpful.

In the extended content, you'll get:
★ Links to Jenn and Ben's Seesaw Author Libraries
★ Direct access to Jenn and Ben's blog
★ Templates and ideas at the EduProtocols website
★ Resources from Lisa Nowakowski's MathReps in Nearpod

tinyurl.com/CallToActionEC
Password: 73468

Want to Learn More about Using EduProtocols in Your Classroom?

Ever wished you could pick the brains of the EduProtocols pioneers? Now you can at EduProtocolsPlus.com!

One price for a lifetime of support!

EduProtocols PLUS

- **Reusable templates** with regular additions
- **Exclusive live and recorded shows** featuring EduProtocols authors and experts
- **Self-paced courses**
- **Supportive community**
- **Discounts** on online, face-to-face PD, and Summer Academies
- **District plans** available

EduProtocolsPLUS.com

EduProtocols books for teaching and leadership

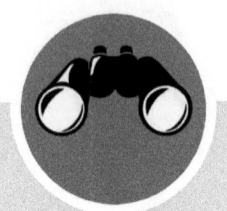

Citations

"Get Started with Design Thinking." Stanford d.school. Retrieved January 8, 2023, from https://dschool.stanford.edu/resources/getting-started-with-design-thinking.

"Rethinking the Classroom for Blended Learning." NEA. Retrieved January 16, 2023, from https://www.nea.org/professional-excellence/student-engagement/tools-tips/rethinking-classroom-blended-learning.

Saint-Exupéry, Antoine. *The Little Prince* (New York: Houghton Mifflin Harcourt, 2000).

Acknowledgments

Ben's Acknowledgements

First, I would like to thank everyone who helped make this book possible. An extra big shoutout to the AMAZING Jennifer Dean, Jon Corripo, Marlena Hebern, Catlin Tucker, and the Dave Burgess crew. Also a big thanks to the EduProtocol group, especially Lisa Nowakowski, Kim Voge, Jacob Carr, Adam Moler, Scott Petri, Josie Wozniak, Ariana Hernandez, Chris Bell, and Jamie Halsey. Among others, these people keep the EduProtocol movement going.

I would also like to thank many local educators who have helped me grow my roots and were with me on a day-to-day basis. Kudos to George Lopez, Jeanne Herrick, Dr. Roberto Nuñez, Dr. Lorie Chamberland, Martin Cisneros, Jonathan Green, Josh Harris, Edi Porter, William Franzell, Lora Carey, Angela Der Ramos, and Yesenia Gutierrez. A round of applause goes to the Kinder Rocket Squad: Veronica, Jessica, Autumn, Jenni, Jasmin, Diana, Monica, and Rocio! I have to give special props to all my #alisalstrong friends and my Monterey Bay CUE peeps, who have been encouraging in this edtech journey. And of course, there is a special place in my heart for all of my students as well.

Thank you to the people in my online PLN who continue to inspire me. I will not list names because there are too many, but know that many of you that are reading this have impacted my life as a teacher. Thanks for sharing your awesome ideas, and thanks to those of you who contributed a testimonial to this book.

Lastly, I would like to thank all my family members who are named at the beginning as well as the ones who aren't, including the Lopez family. And most importantly, I thank God, who has made all of this possible. Praise be to Jesus!

Jenn's Acknowledgements

There are so many people who have helped make this possible. First, I want to thank Jennifer Eyre for encouraging me to get on social media for the purpose of education and find my Professional Learning Network (PLN), who have become like a second family to me. People like Nyree Clark, Tory Wadlington, Sue Thotz, Leticia Citizen, and Toutoule Ntoya from my Equity in Action CA group, who inspire me to reflect and be better every day. Some other major shoutouts to Kim Voge, Jon Corippo, Marlena Hebern, my amazing co-author Benjamin Cogswell, Lisa Nowakowski, and Heather Claborn. I must also include my local Coachella CUE affiliate and friends I have made within CUE.

Additionally, I want to thank every single person who wrote a testimonial or has attended any of our primary EduProtocol professional development sessions. Thanks to all of the amazing people online who are not afraid to try new things and implement EduProtocols in their TK-2 classrooms.

I would also like to thank all the educators at my school who try these crazy ideas with me, help create templates, and do what is best for students. This includes leadership, who not only supports EduProtocols but also helps make integrating them effectively possible. None of this would be possible without my students, who give their all to the creative learning process and make me proud every single day.

Finally, I would like to again thank my family, who have helped encourage me to be the educator I am, supported me along the way, and always helped me follow my dreams and do what is best for kids.

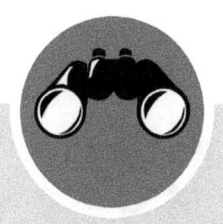

About the Authors

Benjamin Cogwell

Ben Cogswell has been teaching in the Alisal Union School District in Salinas, California, since 2007. Although Ben is currently a kindergarten teacher, he started his journey as a sixth-grade teacher. He loved teaching ancient civilization, pre-algebra, and Harry Potter. When his district adopted 1:1 technology, he saw a new world of possibilities open up.

As a kid of the eighties, Ben had the privilege of growing up with a computer, and he loved fun learning programs like *Math Blaster* and *Kid Pix*. So when he found out he had the opportunity to teach with a class set of iPads, he was over the moon. He enjoyed the challenge of integrating technology into his classroom. Within the first year of 1:1 implementation, the leadership in his district noticed his passion and asked him to step into an educational technology coaching role.

In this role, Ben trained teachers across the school district and introduced programs like Seesaw and Google Classroom, along with education models like the 4Cs and SAMR. Ben built the educational technology department from the ground up and started district-wide technology conferences that are still running to this day. With this experience, he also began presenting at conferences at the state and national level through organizations like CUE. This work has allowed him to collaborate with other edtech leaders including Jon Corripo and learn about EduProtocols.

Although Ben loved coaching, he loved teaching even more and returned to the classroom. As a sixth-grade teacher, Ben witnessed so many students struggling to read that he decided to teach kindergarten. Since 2018, Ben has enjoyed the challenge of shaping young minds, using technology to enhance their learning. He loves seeing students' eyes light up as they learn to read.

Ben received his BA and teaching credential from the University of Pacific and his masters in TESOL from the Middlebury Institute of International Studies. Ben has won several awards, including the Teacher of the Year 2020 from his school district, CUE's Blended and Online Educator of the Year in 2019, the CUE Gold Disk Award in 2023, and the KSBW's Crystal Apple Award. Ben has been featured twice in the *New York Times* and has appeared on MSNBC for his work in the kindergarten classroom. He holds numerous certifications such as Google Innovator, Adobe Innovator, and Seesaw Certified Educator.

Ben currently lives in Salinas, California, with his wife, Jenny, and four children. He loves spending time outdoors hiking and running with his dog and loyal adventure companion, Koko.

Jennifer Dean

When Jenn decided to become a teacher, she knew right away that she wanted to teach in the TK-2 classroom. When she decided to go to college to become a teacher, she enrolled in the early childhood educator program that would give her an Illinois early childhood teaching credential. Jenn is proud of the fact that she completed her entire university experience through online schooling, allowing her to serve as an early childhood paraprofessional in pre-kindergarten classrooms in Illinois, getting hands-on experiences while completing all her coursework. After graduating and receiving her early childhood education certificate from the state of Illinois, Jenn became a full-day pre-kindergarten teacher, where she began to learn and implement best practices such as play-based learning, student agency and voice, cooperative learning strategies, and Universal Design for Learning (UDL).

As she continued her career, she became a second-grade teacher in a beautiful small town called Galena, Illinois. While teaching there, she was introduced to a learning experience platform that was founded on her same beliefs, Seesaw. Jenn began using Seesaw with her students and families and jumped right into the world of integrating technology in ways that supported the 4Cs and UDL and truly fostered a love of learning. She also became a Certified Seesaw Educator. After a great start to her teaching career in Illinois, Jenn and her family decided to move to California, where Jenn continued teaching second grade. There, she continued her passion for teaching in innovative ways and was subsequently introduced to the world of CUE (Computer Using Educators). She began her second masters in instructional technology and became a certified Google Educator and Trainer.

As she dived into this world, she learned more ways to be an innovative teacher who could leverage technology and pedagogy and wanted to share those ideas with others. As a result, she started presenting at local CUE affiliate conferences, as well as the larger Spring CUE conference. By sharing these ideas, she developed a Professional Learning Network (PLN) of like-minded educators. Jenn was named Coachella CUE Outstanding Teacher of the Year in 2018, leading to her eventually becoming the president of the Coachella CUE affiliate. In this role, Jenn was able to bring educators in the Coachella Valley together to collaborate, connect, and create. She was also named Coachella CUE Affiliate Leader of the Year in 2019. This led her to pursue serving CUE at a higher level, becoming a member of the CUE Board in 2022.

Currently, Jenn teaches first grade at Amelia Earhart Elementary School of International Studies in Desert Sands Unified School District in California. She is a mom to a beautiful boy named Jack, a dog named Charleston James, and a cat named California. She is very passionate about meeting the needs of all students, using technology in effective and balanced ways, and of course all things EduProtocols and Seesaw.

More from Dave Burgess Consulting, Inc.

Since 2012, DBCI has published books that inspire and equip educators to be their best. For more information on our titles or to purchase bulk orders for your school, district, or book study, visit DaveBurgessConsulting.com/DBCIbooks.

More from the *Like a PIRATE*™ Series

Teach Like a PIRATE by Dave Burgess
eXPlore Like a PIRATE by Michael Matera
Learn Like a PIRATE by Paul Solarz
Plan Like a PIRATE by Dawn M. Harris
Play Like a PIRATE by Quinn Rollins
Run Like a PIRATE by Adam Welcome
Tech Like a PIRATE by Matt Miller

Lead Like a PIRATE™ Series

Lead Like a PIRATE by Shelley Burgess and Beth Houf
Balance Like a PIRATE by Jessica Cabeen, Jessica Johnson, and Sarah Johnson
Lead beyond Your Title by Nili Bartley
Lead with Appreciation by Amber Teamann and Melinda Miller
Lead with Collaboration by Allyson Apsey and Jessica Gomez
Lead with Culture by Jay Billy
Lead with Instructional Rounds by Vicki Wilson
Lead with Literacy by Mandy Ellis
She Leads by Dr. Rachael George and Majalise W. Tolan

Leadership & School Culture

Beyond the Surface of Restorative Practices by Marisol Rerucha
Change the Narrative by Henry J. Turner and Kathy Lopes
Choosing to See by Pamela Seda and Kyndall Brown
Culturize by Jimmy Casas

Discipline Win by Andy Jacks
Escaping the School Leader's Dunk Tank by Rebecca Coda and Rick Jetter
Fight Song by Kim Bearden
From Teacher to Leader by Starr Sackstein
If the Dance Floor Is Empty, Change the Song by Joe Clark
The Innovator's Mindset by George Couros
It's OK to Say "They" by Christy Whittlesey
Kids Deserve It! by Todd Nesloney and Adam Welcome
Leading the Whole Teacher by Allyson Apsey
Let Them Speak by Rebecca Coda and Rick Jetter
The Limitless School by Abe Hege and Adam Dovico
Live Your Excellence by Jimmy Casas
Next-Level Teaching by Jonathan Alsheimer
The Pepper Effect by Sean Gaillard
Principaled by Kate Barker, Kourtney Ferrua, and Rachael George
The Principled Principal by Jeffrey Zoul and Anthony McConnell
Relentless by Hamish Brewer
The Secret Solution by Todd Whitaker, Sam Miller, and Ryan Donlan
Start. Right. Now. by Todd Whitaker, Jeffrey Zoul, and Jimmy Casas
Stop. Right. Now. by Jimmy Casas and Jeffrey Zoul
Teachers Deserve It by Rae Hughart and Adam Welcome
Teach Your Class Off by CJ Reynolds
They Call Me "Mr. De" by Frank DeAngelis
Thrive through the Five by Jill M. Siler
Unmapped Potential by Julie Hasson and Missy Lennard
When Kids Lead by Todd Nesloney and Adam Dovico
Word Shift by Joy Kirr
Your School Rocks by Ryan McLane and Eric Lowe

Technology & Tools

50 Things to Go Further with Google Classroom by Alice Keeler and Libbi Miller
50 Things You Can Do with Google Classroom by Alice Keeler and Libbi Miller
140 Twitter Tips for Educators by Brad Currie, Billy Krakower, and Scott Rocco
Block Breaker by Brian Aspinall
Building Blocks for Tiny Techies by Jamila "Mia" Leonard
Code Breaker by Brian Aspinall
The Complete EdTech Coach by Katherine Goyette and Adam Juarez

Control Alt Achieve by Eric Curts
The Esports Education Playbook by Chris Aviles, Steve Isaacs, Christine Lion-Bailey, and Jesse Lubinsky
Google Apps for Littles by Christine Pinto and Alice Keeler
Master the Media by Julie Smith
Raising Digital Leaders by Jennifer Casa-Todd
Reality Bytes by Christine Lion-Bailey, Jesse Lubinsky, and Micah Shippee, PhD
Sail the 7 Cs with Microsoft Education by Becky Keene and Kathi Kersznowski
Shake Up Learning by Kasey Bell
Social LEADia by Jennifer Casa-Todd
Stepping Up to Google Classroom by Alice Keeler and Kimberly Mattina
Teaching Math with Google Apps by Alice Keeler and Diana Herrington
Teachingland by Amanda Fox and Mary Ellen Weeks
Teaching with Google Jamboard by Alice Keeler and Kimberly Mattina

Teaching Methods & Materials

All 4s and 5s by Andrew Sharos
Boredom Busters by Katie Powell
The Classroom Chef by John Stevens and Matt Vaudrey
The Collaborative Classroom by Trevor Muir
Copyrighteous by Diana Gill
CREATE by Bethany J. Petty
Deploying EduProtocols by Kim Voge, with Jon Corippo and Marlena Hebern
Ditch That Homework by Matt Miller and Alice Keeler
Ditch That Textbook by Matt Miller
Don't Ditch That Tech by Matt Miller, Nate Ridgway, and Angelia Ridgway
EDrenaline Rush by John Meehan
Educated by Design by Michael Cohen, The Tech Rabbi
The EduProtocol Field Guide by Marlena Hebern and Jon Corippo
The EduProtocol Field Guide: Book 2 by Marlena Hebern and Jon Corippo
The EduProtocol Field Guide: Math Edition by Lisa Nowakowski and Jeremiah Ruesch
The EduProtocol Field Guide: Social Studies Edition by Dr. Scott M. Petri and Adam Moler
Empowered to Choose: A Practical Guide to Personalized Learning by Andrew Easton
Expedition Science by Becky Schnekser
Frustration Busters by Katie Powell
Fully Engaged by Michael Matera and John Meehan
Game On? Brain On! by Lindsay Portnoy, PhD
Guided Math AMPED by Reagan Tunstall

Innovating Play by Jessica LaBar-Twomy and Christine Pinto
Instructional Coaching Connection by Nathan Lang-Raad
Instant Relevance by Denis Sheeran
Keeping the Wonder by Jenna Copper, Ashley Bible, Abby Gross, and Staci Lamb
LAUNCH by John Spencer and A.J. Juliani
Learning in the Zone by Dr. Sonny Magana
Lights, Cameras, TEACH! by Kevin J. Butler
Make Learning MAGICAL by Tisha Richmond
Pass the Baton by Kathryn Finch and Theresa Hoover
Project-Based Learning Anywhere by Lori Elliott
Pure Genius by Don Wettrick
The Revolution by Darren Ellwein and Derek McCoy
The Science Box by Kim Adsit and Adam Peterson
Shift This! by Joy Kirr
Skyrocket Your Teacher Coaching by Michael Cary Sonbert
Spark Learning by Ramsey Musallam
Sparks in the Dark by Travis Crowder and Todd Nesloney
Table Talk Math by John Stevens
Unpack Your Impact by Naomi O'Brien and LaNesha Tabb
The Wild Card by Hope and Wade King
Writefully Empowered by Jacob Chastain
The Writing on the Classroom Wall by Steve Wyborney
You Are Poetry by Mike Johnston
You'll Never Guess What I'm Thinking About by Naomi O'Brien

Inspiration, Professional Growth & Personal Development

Be REAL by Tara Martin
Be the One for Kids by Ryan Sheehy
The Coach ADVenture by Amy Illingworth
Creatively Productive by Lisa Johnson
Educational Eye Exam by Alicia Ray
The EduNinja Mindset by Jennifer Burdis
Empower Our Girls by Lynmara Colón and Adam Welcome
Finding Lifelines by Andrew Grieve and Andrew Sharos
The Four O'Clock Faculty by Rich Czyz
How Much Water Do We Have? by Pete and Kris Nunweiler
P Is for Pirate by Dave and Shelley Burgess

A Passion for Kindness by Tamara Letter
The Path to Serendipity by Allyson Apsey
Recipes for Resilience by Robert A. Martinez
Rogue Leader by Rich Czyz
Sanctuaries by Dan Tricarico
Saving Sycamore by Molly B. Hudgens
The Secret Sauce by Rich Czyz
Shattering the Perfect Teacher Myth by Aaron Hogan
Stories from Webb by Todd Nesloney
Talk to Me by Kim Bearden
Teach Better by Chad Ostrowski, Tiffany Ott, Rae Hughart, and Jeff Gargas
Teach Me, Teacher by Jacob Chastain
Teach, Play, Learn! by Adam Peterson
The Teachers of Oz by Herbie Raad and Nathan Lang-Raad
TeamMakers by Laura Robb and Evan Robb
Through the Lens of Serendipity by Allyson Apsey
The Zen Teacher by Dan Tricarico
Write Here and Now by Dan Tricarico

Children's Books

The Adventures of Little Mickey by Mickey Smith Jr.
Alpert by LaNesha Tabb
Alpert & Friends by LaNesha Tabb
Beyond Us by Aaron Polansky
Cannonball In by Tara Martin
Dolphins in Trees by Aaron Polansky
I Can Achieve Anything by MoNique Waters
I Want to Be a Lot by Ashley Savage
The Magic of Wonder by Jenna Copper, Ashley Bible, Abby Gross, and Staci Lamb
Micah's Big Question by Naomi O'Brien
The Princes of Serendip by Allyson Apsey
Ride with Emilio by Richard Nares
A Teacher's Top Secret Confidential by LaNesha Tabb
A Teacher's Top Secret: Mission Accomplished by LaNesha Tabb
The Wild Card Kids by Hope and Wade King
Zom-Be a Design Thinker by Amanda Fox